Coast to Coast

C2C
Hadrian's Cycleway
Reivers

14th Edition

By Mark Porter with John Grimshaw

Accommodation, Food and Drink
History, Route and Maps
In the
Lake District, Pennines and Scottish Borders

By: Mark Porter
Design: Hayley Hunter
Copyright: Baytree Press ©

Published by:
Baytree Press,
Bridge Street, Rothbury,
Northumberland NE65 7SG

+44 (0) 7767 893790
info@c2c-guide.co.uk
www.c2c-accommodation.co.uk

ISBN: 978-0-9555082-3-3

Coast to Coast

Cycle Routes

Accommodation, Food and Drink
History, Route and Maps over three great Sea to
Sea rides in the Lake District, Pennines and Borders

C2C
Hadrian's Cycleway
Reivers

by Mark Porter with John Grimshaw

14th Edition

Contents

Introduction

2009 is the 15th anniversary of the C2C, Britain's most popular and best known cycle route. It also marks the 14th edition of this publication. The revamped guide, now also containing a full low-down on Hadrian's Cycleway, will give you even better information in an even more user-friendly format. As well as being a west to east route, the Hadrian's is ideal for those going east to west, and that is the way we have laid out the pages.

Much of the information in this book is also on our website www.c2c-guide.co.uk which will now also host the new Hadrian and Reivers websites, giving riders and advertisers an even wider spread of information. You can also purchase commemorative T-shirts and Sustrans maps covering a variety of routes on the website. But unlike a pocket book, it is hard to stuff a website in your pocket, so the book retains its usefulness even in this electronic era.

There is something about propelling oneself from one side of Britain to the other which captures the imagination. It is an easily quantifiable achievement – just like Land's End to John O'Groats, but on a more manageable scale. It combines the majesty of the Northern Lakes, whose charms are much the same as in Wordsworth's day, with the beauty of the Eden Valley, and the challenge of the Pennines.

These coast to coast rides have everything you could want, holding appeal to expert and beginner alike; and all can be managed over a long weekend. The daddy of them all, the C2C, was set up by the cycling charity Sustrans and this guide is designed to be used with the C2C Sustrans Map, obtainable from the National Cycle Network Centre or from www.c2c-guide.co.uk.

National Cycle Network Centre,
Cathedral Square, College Green,
Bristol BS1 5DD
0845 113 0065
For speed:
PO Box 21, Bristol BS99 2HA
You can also get it from tourist
information centres or via the website:

www.sustrans.org.uk

Hadrian's Cycleway

Since it was launched three summers ago Hadrian's Cycleway has proved a tremendous pull for cyclists. For those wishing to voyage coast to coast twice in one trip, it is an ideal way of heading east to west, to the start of the C2C, bringing you back to your start point on the east coast.

Reivers maps: Unit 87, Stirling Enterprise Park, Stirling, FK7 7RP
01786 479886
www.footprintmaps.co.uk.

Your hosts on all three rides have been chosen for their understanding of the cyclist's needs, a warm welcome, acceptance of muddy legs, a secure place for your bike and provision of a meal either with them or at a nearby pub. The C2C is designed to be tackled west to east to take advantage of the prevailing winds. Both the Sustrans map and this accommodation guide run from west to east, so Hadrian's Cycleway or the Reivers can be treated as a 'return' leg for those brave enough to tackle the whole circuit. They are both ideal for an east-west crossing of the UK.

Please try to book accommodation, meals and packed lunches in advance, and do not arrive unannounced expecting beds and meals to be available. If you have to cancel a booking, please give the proprietor as much notice as you can so that the accommodation can be re-let. Your deposit may be forfeited: this is at the discretion of the proprietor. Suggestions for additional addresses are most welcome, together with your comments. We are particularly keen to receive reports about the efficacy of waymarking on both routes, and comments (both positive and adverse) on our route tips and guidance.

*Please note that the information given in the guide was correct at the time of printing and was as supplied by the proprietors. No responsibility can be accepted by this independent company as to the completeness or accuracy of all entries, nor for any loss arising as a result. It is advisable to check the relevant details when booking.

Foreword

This small guide is essential reading for everyone who would like to explore the north by bicycle. The C2C route from Whitehaven and Workington to Sunderland and Newcastle was opened in 1994 and remains the country's most popular and iconic cycle route, seen as a challenge to cycle its 140 miles in one day, but for most of us as a memorable way of crossing outstanding countryside in easy stages. The Reivers route through the wilder Northumberland countryside was opened a few years later and then in 2006 the Sustrans Summer Trailblazing Ride opened Hadrian's Cycle Way in the hottest weather imaginable. The Solway was like liquid gold and the sunsets mirrored Turner's pictures.

This expanded guide comes at an opportune time. Never before has there been so great a need to encourage us to holiday at home and to travel without a car. Transport accounts for a significant proportion of all climate change emissions and tourism for half of that. A week cycling across the country and even better another week back again, instead of holidaying abroad, will make the most significant contribution within your power to tackling this pressing problem.

Of course when you are cycling these routes, whether it is the C2C, Hadrian's or Reivers, you are not thinking much about these wider issues but rather the effort to keep going, the reward at the end of the day and the memories which will be as vivid as any you could have had in a far flung corner of the world.

John Grimshaw, CBE
President of SUSTRANS

The route

The C2C is designed to be cycled from west coast to east coast. This is because of prevailing winds and gradients: do it this way and, god-willing, the wind will be behind you and most of the climbs will be short and sharp, rather than long and grinding. East to west is for those who like unrelentingly hostile gradients with the wind in their face. If you want to cycle east to west, a more user-friendly route is the Reivers or Hadrian's Cycleway (see elsewhere in this guide).

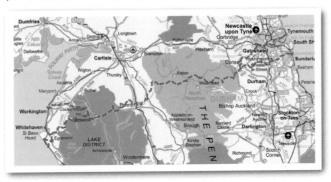

Acknowledgements

Many thanks to John Grimshaw (CBE and President of Sustrans). John is my co-author for the new Hadrian's Cycleway section of the book. He and his erstwhile colleague David Gray were instrumental in building the C2C. Some of their images have been reproduced on the following pages, along with those of Anthea Truby, Martin Herron, Julia Bayne, Barry Wilson, Pat Strachan, G.L. Jones and Steve Morgan.

Thanks also to Newcastle Gateshead Initiative, the Cumbria Tourist Board picture library, Footprint Maps for their co-operation with the splendid Reivers route, and **www.thecumbriadirectory.com**, whose website provided occasional background information.

SUSTRANS stands for sustainable transport. It is a charity which is in the process of turning many of Britain's minor byways and pathways into a national network of cycle routes as part of a crusade to encourage us to use the combustion engine less. It has transformed 10,000 miles of old road, track and pathway into the National Cycle Network, of which the C2C is a small but important part. If you would like to become a member of Sustrans you can do so by writing to them.

Getting there

Train

There are three choices of start, and two choices of finish. All three possible starts, **Whitehaven**, **Workington** and **Egremont & St Bees** are accessible by train on the local First North Western line from Carlisle. The journey follows the spectacular, dramatic coastline and takes about an hour. Remember to book your bike on in advance.

There is a cross country service to **Carlisle**, where you pick up the connection to the starting point of choice. I have heard reports of the rail services being unhelpful to cyclists but I gather there has been a big change in attitude and they are now altogether more helpful – though this is at the discretion of the guard or ticket inspector.

Sunderland Station
There is a ban on taking bicycles on the Tyne and Wear Metro, but they are carried by the other train operators from Sunderland Station.
It's on the regional link between Newcastle and Middlesbrough/Darlington.
Cyclists are welcome on Grand Central trains from London to Sunderland via the Durham Heritage Coast and York.

National Rail Enquiries: 08457 484950
First North Western: 08457 000125
(sales)
Virgin Trains (West Coast): 08457 222333
There are excellent services to get you
home direct from Newcastle Central
Station, (pictured)
Direct line: 0191 221 3156
National Express: 08457 225225

Air

Newcastle Airport is only 20
minutes from the city centre
and there are regular and
frequent links to many major
European cities, including
Amsterdam, Brussels and
Paris, along with international
connections to the rest of the
world. Within the UK, there are
also direct flights to Aberdeen,
Birmingham, Gatwick,
Heathrow, Wick, Dublin and
Belfast.
0191 286 0966
www.newcastleairport.com

Sea

The International Ferry
Terminal
at Royal Quays is the North
of England's main sea link
with Continental Europe with
regular passenger services
from Amsterdam's ferry
terminal in the Netherlands.
It is an ideal start point for
the Reivers, Hadrian's Wall
or C2C in reverse if you don't
fancy getting the train across
to Whitehaven, Workington
or St Bees & Egremont.
DFDS Seaways
0191 293 6262

Taxi

Motorised alternatives, in the form of specialist taxi services, are readily available for the return journey. Some of them will organise the whole package for you.

The Bike Bus, Stanley Mini Coaches, Stanley: 01207 237424

Cycle Active, Langwathby: 01768 881111

Tyne Valley Holidays, Newcastle: 0191 284 7534

Car

All three starting points are easily accessible by road.
From the south and east: take the M6 to Penrith, where you pick up the A66 through Keswick to your chosen starting point. The road goes straight into Workington, or turn onto the A595 at Bridgefoot for Whitehaven or Egremont.
From the north: Head to Carlisle, leaving the city on the A595. For Workington, turn onto the A596 at Thursby. Stick with the road you are on for Whitehaven or Egremont.

Most accommodation owners will allow you to leave your vehicle with them. Or you may prefer a secure long-term car park. There is one in the centre of Whitehaven.

There is £3-a-day parking one mile from the start of the C2C at one of the last mile points on the home leg of the Reivers Route, run by a Sustrans ranger, no less.
Contact Jim Hewitson
01946 692178
In Workington, there's parking at the quayside for £2.50 a day:
Contact Martin Perkins
01900 604997

For further information call the Tourist Information Centre:
Whitehaven:
01946 852939
Workington:
01900 606699
Back-up vehicles are kindly requested to use main roads in order to keep the C2C route as traffic-free as possible.

Way Marking

The route is
waymarked with a
blue direction sign
complete with the
letters C2C and a
red number 7 – the
number of the route.
These are posted

at junctions and other strategic spots. Occasionally the road
surface is signed; sometimes there are just little plastic stickers
posted to gates and lamp-posts. Signage is not always brilliant,
but with sharp eyes and the use of a map you should not get
lost. Having said that, sections at the beginning and end are
notorious for the lack of signs; vandals like to trash them and
souvenir hunters snaffle them.

Maps

There is basic mapping in this guide, along with topographical
maps showing profiles of such beastly climbs as Hartside. You
will also need the Sustrans C2C map. If you want to, take the
Ordnance Survey maps but they are bulky and the waymarking
means they are unnecessary. You could also invest in the OS
Interactive Atlas, and download or print the relevant sections.
The two-CD option costs around £30.

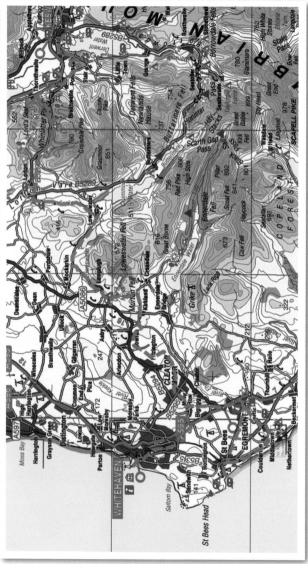

Ordnance Survey © Crown copyright: 100039985

Egremont to Keswick

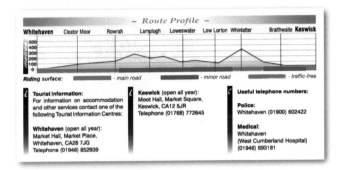

~ Route Profile ~

| Whitehaven | Cleator Moor | Rowrah | Lamplugh | Loweswater | Low Lorton | Whinlatter | Braithwaite | Keswick |

Riding surface: ■ - main road   ■ - minor road   ■ - traffic-free

Tourist Information:
For information on accommodation and other services contact one of the following Tourist Information Centres:

Whitehaven (open all year):
Market Hall, Market Place,
Whitehaven, CA28 7JG
Telephone (01946) 852939

Keswick (open all year):
Moot Hall, Market Square,
Keswick, CA12 5JR
Telephone (01768) 772645

Useful telephone numbers:

Police:
Whitehaven (01900) 602422

Medical:
Whitehaven
(West Cumberland Hospital)
(01946) 693181

Whitehaven

Departure Route

- As you leave Whitehaven harbour you will join the Whitehaven-Rowrah cycle path, which links the sea to the fells.
- First, detailed instructions for getting onto the route proper:
  Out of the harbour head right up Quay Street.
- Left past the Tourist Information Centre through Market Place and into Preston Street. Look out for signs on the left for the path behind Focus DIY.
- Onto Esk Avenue, only to rejoin the path by the school. You then cycle along Croasdale Avenue and Wasdale Avenue before linking up with the path to exit the town.
- You now follow the railway line built in the 1850s to carry limestone, coal and iron; it is now a sculpture trail interpreting the geology and industrial history of the region. You might find yourself stopping to check signage; this is routine, there are several other routes around here including the Egremont link.

Cycle Shops

Haven Cycles, Cycle Hire/Repairs, Preston St Garage **01946 63263.** havencycles@yahoo.co.uk Only 500 metres from start, offering cycle hire, repairs, accessories and cycle sales. Secure car parking, now offering a complete package of baggage transfer, hire cycle collection and transport back from the finish if required.

About the town

Whitehaven has the distinction of being both the starting point of the C2C and the finish for the Reivers Cycle Route. It may not be quite the place it was in the 18th century, when it played a significant role in the British slave industry and was the main importer of tobacco on the west coast, but it has undergone a major transformation in the last couple of years and its fine Georgian architecture is now looking spruce and proud again.

Perhaps the most impressive feature is the large harbour, which has undergone a £68 million facelift. There is a fine 100-berth marina, now choc-a-bloc with pleasure craft of all sizes and shapes. The town has, in short, re-acquired some of the prosperity it lost in the years after it became the world's first new town.

Not so long ago it would have been hard to imagine that early Manhattan's street grid system was based on the pattern the Lowther family laid out for Whitehaven in the late 1690s, when it became apparent that the Cumbrian settlement was destined for great things.

Shortly afterwards the streets filled with rum and sugar merchants, slave traders and tobacco speculators as well as America-bound settlers waiting for their boat to come and take them off to a new life in the New World. The harbour was teeming with coal transporters, which plied the Irish Sea to supply Dublin's houses and industries with black stuff dynamited from under Whitehaven's seabed.

There was also shipbuilding; more than 1,000 vessels were built in the Whitehaven yards, and one of the oldest surviving iron-built ships was constructed here. After London and Bristol, this was the busiest port in England.

Places of Interest

The Beacon (01946 592302)
Local maritime and industrial history within the Harbour Gallery and magnificent views over the town. Done up during 2007.

Michael Moon's Bookshop & Gallery (01946 599010), 19 Lowther St.
One of the largest bookshops in Cumbria, "vast and gloriously eccentric!"

The Rum Story (01946 592933), Lowther Street.
Exhibition celebrating the Jefferson family business, the oldest booze empire in Britain.

The Haig Mining Museum (01946 599949)
Solway Road, Kells, Whitehaven.
Memories of the last deep pit in Cumbria.

American Links

Whitehaven's connections with America go deep: John Paul Jones, founder of the American navy and erstwhile scourge of Britain's own, gained his sea legs as a merchant seaman from Whitehaven. Indeed, the last invasion of the English mainland, in 1778, was perpetrated by Jones upon the town. The incursion was part of the only attack on British soil by US forces; and we should not forget that George Washington's granny, Mildred Warner Gale, lived here and is buried at St Nicholas's churchyard.

The town has been impressively preserved, one suspects, because a sudden lack of prosperity after the boom years disinclined planners from bulldozing in the name of progress. This left the Lowther architectural heritage preserved, as it were, in aspic. It is worthwhile walking the streets, admiring this memorial to an earlier and prosperous age, when sea captains and merchants lived in style. There are many interesting and quirky sculptures around the harbour, a number of street mosaics featuring different aspects of the town's heritage, plus a mural in Washington Square and a plethora of shiny plaques above doorways giving clues to the past. It is one of my favourite places on the whole route and it seems a shame just to use Whitehaven as a point of departure without spending the previous night exploring. There are plenty of distractions, in the form of pubs, restaurants and venues. The following day's ride out of this port is nothing if not leisurely - a stark contrast to the undulations that are to follow. A late night is not going to spoil it.

The traditional way to start this route is by christening your bike on the slipway behind the big C2C sign by dipping the front wheel in the briny. Then you might wish to get your first route stamp at the New Espresso café in the Market Place.

Where to eat

The Vagabond, 9 Marlborough Street. **01946 693671**
Georgian House, Church Street. **01946 696611**
Casa Romana, Queen Street. **01946 591901**
Jasmine Palace, Duke/Strand Street. **0871 5297754**
Blue Wine Bar & Restaurant, Tangier Street. **01946 691986**
Westminster Coffee Bar, Lowther Street. **01946 694404**
Askash Tandoori. **01946 691171**
Ali Taj Restaurant , 34/35 Tangier St. **01946 592679**
Howgate Brewster & Travel Inn. **01946 66286**
Zest Harbourside. **01946 66981**
The Wellington Bistro, at the Beacon (see page 14), **01946 590231**

Accommodation

The Mansion, Old Woodhouse, Whitehaven, Cumbria CA28 9LN
Run by: Tom Todd & Philip Kirkbride
Friendly, relaxed and with all mod cons. Super big screen TV and
swimming pool opening this year.
12 rooms.
B&B: £25-£30.
Pk Lunch: £3.50.
Eve Meal: £6-£10.
Nr pub: 100m.
Dist to C2C: 0.5 miles.
01946 61860/01946 691270
comnenus4@aol.com
www.themansion–whitehaven.co.uk

Glenfield Guest House, Whitehaven, Cumbria, CA28 7TS
Run by: Margaret & Andrew Davies
Set in a conservation area close to the town centre but with a home-
from-home atmosphere. Specialises in home cooking and luxury
en-suite accommodation. Licensed lounge with open fire. Free WiFi
and on-line booking.
Rooms: 1S, 2D, 1T, 2F
£30-£35, Twin £55.
Eve Meal: £7.50.
Pk Lunch: £4.50.
Nr pub: 50m.
Dist to C2C: 400m.
AA 4-star. Welcome to Excellence Award.
4 star Food Safety Performance.
01946 691911
www.glenfield–whitehaven.co.uk
glenfieldGH@aol.com

Chestnuts, Low Moresby, Whitehaven, Cumbria, CA28 6RX
Run by: Norah Messenger

You can leave your car here for the duration at this private home with newly refurbished bedroom, king-sized bed and modern en-suite shower room. Small village north of Whitehaven, safe and secure parking for cars and cycles, peaceful garden where you can enjoy a relaxing evening watching owls in their aviaries before a refreshing night's sleep and good breakfast to set you up for your journey.

Rooms: 2D- 2Bunks.
B&B: £25.
Pk lunch: from £4.50.
Secure Cycle parking.
Pub 5 minutes walk on footpath.
01946 61612
owlmagic@tesco.net
www.chestnuts-whitehaven.com

Glenard Guest House, Inkerman Terr, Whitehaven, CA28 7TY
Run by: Mrs. E. Armstrong

Large detached family run Victorian Guest House set in its own grounds. Breakfasts from 6am for those wishing for an early start. Secure cycle storage. 0.25 from start of C2C.

Rooms: 2D, 2S, 2T, 3F.
B&B: from £25.
Pk lunch: £4.
Nr pub: 5min walk.
Dist to C2C: 0.5 miles.
01946 692249
info@glenard.co.uk
www.glenard.co.uk

Tarn Flatt Barn, Tarn Flatt Hall, Sandwith, Whitehaven CA28 9UX
Run by: Janice Telfer

Traditional sandstone barn on a working farm. 1 mile from Sandwith and 3 miles from Whitehaven. Basic communal accommodation for 13 visitors. Sleeping on raised wooden platform, coin operated shower. 2 WCs. Wood burning stove. Parking for cars and bikes, also long stay parking available.

Bed only: £7.
Open: all year.
Secure cycle parking.
Distance from route: 3 miles.
Pub: 1 mile away.
01946 692162
stay@tarnflattfarm.co.uk
www.tarnflattfarm.co.uk

19

Chase Hotel, Inkerman Terrace, Whitehaven CA28 8AA

Run by: Duty Mananger

Car parking for duration privately owned Victorian former
gentleman's residence in two acres of grounds. Quiet and
comfortable with plenty of parking space, a short stroll from the town
centre. Cyclists are welcome to leave their bikes for the duration in
a secure lock-up for bikes. Has been looking after C2Cers since the
route opened.

Rooms: 23. 6S, 4T, 13D.
B&B: from £25 for groups of 10.
or more; Twins/doubles £65.
Evening meal: £7 - £15.
Packed lunch: from £5.
Fully licensed.
0.25 miles from route.
Town centre: 0.25 miles.
01946 693656 / 01946 590807
www.chasewhitehaven.co.uk
chase1@tms–connect.co.uk

Read Guest House, 5 Cross St, Whitehaven, CA28 7BX

Run by: Jacky & Ann Walker

Elegant 18th century house in the town centre offering 10 twin
rooms well suited for groups. Ideal at weekends as it tends to be
booked during the week. This house - in fact two houses knocked
into one - was built by the Whitehaven artist, Mathias Read, whose
paintings captured much of the town's splendour in its Georgian
heyday. Surrounded by pubs and restaurants, this is an ideal start
point for weekend C2Cers.

Rooms: 10T.
B&B: £25. No single occupancy tariff.
Secure bike storage.
Restaurant and pubs all round.
Distance from start 200m.
01946 61515 or 07771 553819
ukbsolutions@msn.com

Waverley Hotel, Tangier St, CA28 7UX

Run by: Cheryl Twinn

Bustling privately owned town centre
hotel, traditional in style, licensed and
with busy restaurant. Close to harbour
and popular amongst cyclists.

Rooms: 10S, 5D,6T,3F.
From £55T. £68D. £30-£55 single. Fam
(3) £70. Fam (4) £75.
Eve Meal: £5.95-£15.
Pk Lunch: from £5.95.
Fully Licensed.
Dist to C2C: On route.
01946 694337
www.thewaverleyhotel.co.uk
thewaverleyhotel@hotmail.com

Cleator Moor & Ennerdale

Alternative First Night

Ideal stop-over places for those arriving later in the day at Whitehaven or St Bees. You can dip your wheels in the sea at Whitehaven (5 miles) or St Bees (7 miles) then have a gentle ride to acclimatise for those bigger challenges facing you over the next few days. This also gets around possible accommodation log-jams in Whitehaven or St Bees (or Workington, for that matter). Ennerdale Bridge, a lovely rural village with two pubs and a shop, is about a mile to the east of the route at Kirkland (you can head straight there out of Cleator Moor or simply turn right at Kirkland). Cleator Moor, meanwhile, boasts an Indian and Chinese restaurant (both pretty good) plus a fine budget cafe. See details below.

Ennerdale village spans the River Ehen and is close to Ennerdale Water, the most westerly of the lakes (and the most remote - it is the only lake which has no road running alongside). Here lies one of the largest forests in Cumbria in the Ennerdale Valley, with more than 20 miles of forest road plus a tangle of footpaths open to the public. The village is only a short hop from the C2C (also known as the West Cumbria Cyclepath). Wainwright's Coast to Coast Walk travels through Cleator before reaching Ennerdale village, so the village is a popular stopping off point on the route.

Forged in the red heat of old technology, Cleator Moor is a creation of the Industrial Revolution. The era's insatiable need for more coal, limestone and iron ore meant that the village became a town, which developed rapidly in the 19th century. As did the villages around it: Frizington, Rowrah, Keekle, Bigrigg produced the raw materials for iron works in Cleator Moor and Workington. To service this hive of industrial activity there was also an intricate network of railways, known as the Cleator & Workington junction railway.

The town's nickname was 'Little Ireland', owing to the influx of workers from across the water. World War I and World War II saw a fresh influx of migrant workers from the ravages of mainland Europe and in 1938 Jakob Spreiregen founded the company Kangol in Cleator, situated across the road from St Mary's Church. The original factory building still stands though manufacturing has since transferred to the Kangol factory in China. Although manufacturing on the site has ended, the factory shop remains open for business and there are talks of redeveloping the site as a tourist attraction.

Accommodation

Parkside Hotel, Parkside Road, Cleator Moor, CA28 5HB

Run by: John Bruckshaw

A friendly, affordable, family run hotel, ideally placed for the C2C and on the edge of the Lake District National Park. Perfect place for those who might be tempted to stay and explore the beautiful Western Lakes and Fells or the Solway Coast. En-suite rooms plus real ales and home-cooked bar meals.

Rooms: 2T/D, 2F, 1S, 1Tpl.

B&B: £29.50 - £39. £25 each for triple.

Eve meal: £6.95-£13.95.

Pk lunch: £3.50-£4.95.

On route. Real Ales.

01946 811001

www.parksidehotelcumbria.co.uk

enquiries@parksidehotelcumbria.co.uk

Shepherds Arms Hotel, Ennerdale Bridge, Ennerdale, CA23 3AR

This is an ideal stop-off for those arriving by train or car later in the day. It is seven miles from the start at Whitehaven and/or St Bees, so is a splendid way of easing into the ride and is only a mile from the route, near Kirkland. This is a small gem of a country hotel with public bar serving real ales and pub meals. Situated on the famous Coast to Coast walk, the area is fast becoming popular with cyclists using the new start. A busy local pub with comfortable rooms.

Rooms: 3D, 3T, 2D/T.

B&B: £39.50-£49.50.

Eve meal: under £10 for a main course.

Pk lunch: £3.95-£5.50.

01946 861249

www.shepherdsarmshotel.co.uk

shepherdsarms@btconnect.com

The Fox & Hounds, Ennerdale Bridge, CA23 3AR

Run by: Malcolm Thomas-Chapman

Comfortable and cosy country pub serving real ale and good food. Malcolm, who runs the nearby Shepherds Arms, recently took over and now runs both of the village's pubs. Great place to stop off if you want to have an easy first day having maybe arrived in the afternoon at the start.

Rooms: 2D, 1T.

B&B: £39.50 - £49.50.

Eve meal: under £10 for main course.

Pk lunch: £3.95 - £5.50.

Secure cycle lock-up. 1 mile from route.

01946 861181

www.shepherdsarmshotel.co.uk

shepherdsarms@btconnect.com

St Bees & Egremont

By popular request we decided in 2007 to introduce a third possible start to the route: St Bees, the seaside neighbour of the newly vibrant Egremont. St Bees is the tried and trusted start to the Coast to Coast walk, famously founded by Alfred Wainwright in 1973. It is also a lovely coastal setting and a splendid but smaller alternative to the bustling charms of Whitehaven and Workington. The Egremont area has been mining iron ore and quarrying for more than 800 years and it is home to Florence Mine, the last deep Iron Ore mine in Western Europe.

There is plenty of eager and competitive accommodation in Egremont, plus numerous hostelries and eateries in the area. Indeed, huge efforts are being put into the regeneration of this former weaving and dyeing town.
Egremont's hidden gems include the Norman Castle with its literary connection to Wordsworth's Ballad of the Horn of Egremont; Hartley's ice cream factory and shop; Lowes Court Gallery and its Tourist Information Centre, **01946 820693**, with exhibitions of Cumbrian artists and local crafts.
As a 'Fairtrade Town' Egremont has a number of shops selling locally produced and sourced foods and holds a Farmers Market on the third Friday of every month in the Market Hall.The main street has a variety of facilities, shops, pubs and takeaways catering for visitor needs.

During the annual Crab Fair, which celebrated its 840th anniversary in September 2007, the greasy pole climbing and gurning (face pulling) events draw large crowds of locals and visitors. Indeed, the town is synonymous with that time honoured English tradition of gurning.

This year will see further improvements to the town and its facilities, such as circular cycling routes, riverside walks and new planting to the town's entrances as part of the Egremont Market Town Initiative work.
The Tourist Information Centre at Lowes Court Gallery is always there for details of things to do in and around the town. **01946 820693**

The local regeneration partnership is keen to improve the visitor offer further and welcomes your comments, suggestions and information by email, through its website or by post: regeneration@VisitEgremont.co.uk
www.virtualegremont.co.uk
De Lucy Centre, 15 Market Place, Egremont, CA22 2AF
01946 828 101 or **07795 290826**

Directions

St Bees to merge point with Whitehaven route

- Those arriving at St Bees by train should leave the station to the Priory Church side and make their way along the 'Coach Road' past the petrol station and garage to the beach.
- St Bees Head is the most westerly point in the North of England and on a clear day from the promenade you can look out to the Isle of Man, 20 miles or so off the coast.
- The first stage of the route takes you to Egremont, four miles away. Leave the beach car park and take the first right along the straight road to the Station. Cross the level crossing and continue up the Main Street past the Platform 9 restaurant and the Queens Hotel on your right, the Manor House Hotel and the post office on your left.
- At the next junction you have the choice to take:
  The challenging route left up Outrigg (20%) and over Baybarrow, with rewarding views over to Ennerdale, Wasdale and down the coast to Eskdale and further
- Or continue up the Main Street to take the second right – signposted for the Hadrians Way C72 route – and follow the coast (Nethertown Road) and charming single-track lanes to Coulderton, then head inland for Egremont and the Lakes.
- At the T-junction in Coulderton head right to Middletown, taking first left just before the telephone box. Follow the lane for a short while, but instead of heading right, go straight on past Black Ling and Pickett How, up the narrow minor road. Make sure to enjoy views across to Dent Fell – the western edge of the Lake District as you head towards Egremont. Arriving in Egremont, take time to visit the Castle (pictured), then follow the national cycle route 72 which is clearly signed through the town and out to the north.

- About a mile north of Egremont is Clintz Quarry Nature Reserve, a limestone quarry of dramatic proportions with 100ft cliffs. It is home to some rare orchids in May and June, and is a sanctuary for birds.

Accommodation

Stone House Farm, Main St, St Bees, CA27 0DE

Run by: Carole Smith

Secure bike storage On route for C2C and Hadrian's Cycleway
Friendly family run bed and breakfast in a large modernised Georgian
farmhouse in the centre of the village, near the railway station and
local shops, restaurants and hotels. Only three minutes' ride from the
start of the C2C (not to mention Wainwright's coast to coast walk).
Full English breakfast and free parking. There is, however, a charge
for long stay car parking of £2.50 per night.

Rooms: 1S, 2T, 1F 2D, 1Tpl.
B&B: £30-£35.
Evening meal: local pubs & hotels.
Pk lunch: £5.
01946 822224
www.stonehousefarm.net
csmith.stonehouse@btopenworld.com

Horse & Groom, Market Place, Court, Egremont CA22 2AE

Run by: Rob Merrett

In the town centre, in the middle of the Western Lakes, Horse &
Groom offers budget en-suite accommodation for families, walkers
and cyclists. Self-catering and there are plenty of shops, pubs and
restaurants nearby. Secure lock-up and cleaning facilities.

Rooms: 1 six bed dorm, 1Q, 3T.
All en-suite wet rooms
Bed: £8
Self-catering or surrounding pubs
and restaurants.
Sleeping bags for hire: £2.
01946 758198
www.horseandgroomcourt.co.uk
info@horseandgroomcourt.co.uk

Albert Hotel, 1 Finkle St, St Bees, Cumbria, CA27 0BN

Clean and well run hotel at the bottom of Main St. A popular pub
as well, with a pleasant beer garden. Carole, the owner, obviously
loves her job and the atmosphere is as warm as a steak pie. Secure
storage and whopping breakfasts for those who like a challenging
start. Astonishing value and very tidy rooms, all with Georgian sash
windows.

Rooms: 2D, 3T, 2S.
B&B: £25 (there is no extra charge
for single occupancy).
Evening meals: yes for groups or those
coinciding with groups. Around £4.50.
Packed lunch: £3.
01946 822345

Platform 9 Restaurant & B&B, The Old Station House, Main St, St Bees, Cumbria CA27 0DG

Charming location at the start of the route with a good restaurant and a beer garden. There are three rooms and lots of restaurant choice, from bar snacks to a la carte. Chef Martin Allison has had two AA rosettes. Secure storage for bikes. Great place to start from.

Rooms: 2D, 1T.
B&B: £32.50-£45.
DB&B: £75 (for two, weekend only).
Evening meal: £7.95-£19.95.
Pk lunch: £4.75.
01946 822600
stuart@platform9.co.uk
www.platform9.co.uk

Queens Hotel, Main St, St Bees, Cumbria, CA27 0DE

Run by: Mark Smedley

17th century hotel with a cosy country pub atmosphere, with oak beams and log fires. There are two real ale bars and a decent wine list. The restaurant has been comfortably and tastefully refurbished and all meals are cooked on the premises using locally sourced ingredients where possible. Large conservatory and terraced garden. Secure cycle storage.

Rooms: 7 rooms currently available (7 more to follow).
B&B: £26-£38.
Evening meal: from £6.95.
Pk lunch: from £5.95.
01946 822287
www.queenshotelstbees.co.uk
enquiries@queenshotelstbees.co.uk

Fairladies Barn Guest House, Main St, St Bees, Cumbria CA27 0AD

Run by: Will & Nicola Corrie

Beautiful 17th century sandstone barn that looks as if it has been transported from one of those picture postcard villages in the Dordogne. Luxury accommodation at affordable prices.

Rooms: 4D, 3T, 2F (1D & 1T with shared bathroom).
B&B: £30-£40.
Evening meal: Lots of nearby pubs.
Pk lunch: £5.50.
01946 822718
www.fairladiesbarn.co.uk
info@fairladiesbarn.co.uk

Lorton

Directions
Merging of the routes to Lorton

- Whether you have come up the disused railway line from Whitehaven or joined the main cycle route from Egremont, the next stage sees you cut through Cleator Moor and rejoin the old railway heading towards Rowrah and Kirkland.
- Beyond Rowrah turn left onto the lane and right at the school. You will soon pass Felldyke where you follow the signs for Lamplugh and Loweswater.
- In about 5km you will be skirting the Loweswater lake, your first glimpse of the Lakes and a wonderful spot to take pictures or stop for a snack. Beyond is the picturesque village of Loweswater, complete with church and village inn, a delightful place to stop if you are really taking your time, or are on foot.
- Head left at Loweswater, up the lane through Thackthwaite and soon you will cross the River Cocker at Low Lorton, passing through Lorton Vale and into High Lorton. This is a truly picturesque Northern Lakes village to spend a night.

On Arrival

Alfred Wainwright, Britain's most famous walking hero and pioneer of the outdoors, regarded this area, with its deeply gouged valleys reached from the passes of Whinlatter, Honister and Newlands, as his favourite spot.

Lorton is only about 5km south of Cockermouth, so it is also an optional diversion for those who have decided to start their journey from Workington.

To reach New House (see p.28) on the B5289:

Carry on straight through Loweswater for 3km on the road parallel with the route:

Turn right onto the B5289 at the cross-roads just beyond the Lorton bridge. It's only 2km from the route.

Accommodation

New House Farm, Lorton, Cockermouth, Cumbria CA139UU

Run by: Hazel Thompson

Award winning 17th century grade II listed farmhouse set in stunning surroundings, now boasting a tea room with delicious home-made produce. Beautiful antiques throughout complement the original oak beams, flag floors and stone fireplaces where log fires crackle on colder days. Four posters, hot tub in the garden. Delicious food.

Rooms: 5D, 1T (E-S).
B&B: £80.
Pk lunch: £7.50.
Eve meal: £24 for 3 courses.
Distance from route: 1 mile.
VisitBritain 5 stars. Which?
Hotel of the year award winner.
Pub 1.5 miles.
Tea room now available
01900 85404 (07841 159818)
www.newhouse-farm.com
enquiries@newhouse-farm.co.uk

Winder Hall Country House, Low Lorton, Cockermouth, CA13 9UP

Run by: Ann and Nick Lawler

Beautiful hideaway in a historic manor house just off C2C. A popular stopping point for sandwiches and coffee before the tough climb up Whinlatter. Also popular for afternoon teas and a good resting place for those who like to take things easy. Indeed, not a bad overnight for anyone coming back along the Reivers (about 3 miles south of the route down the B5292). The rooms are very pretty and the food is organic and excellent.

Rooms: 7D, 2T, 2F, 2 four-posters.
B&B: £51-90.
Eve Meal: £27-£39.
Distance from C2C: 100m.
5 Diamonds. Fine Dining Award.
01900 85107 | 01900 85479
www.winderhall.co.uk
stay@winderhall.co.uk

Meadow Bank, High Lorton, Cockermouth, Cumbria CA13 9UG

Run by: Christine Edmunds

The reception here is as warm as the rooms and the location could hardly be bettered. Secure bike storage, drying facilities, pub close by and a great breakfast to see you on your way.

Rooms: 1D, 1T (E-S).
B&B: £26-£28.
Pk Lunch: £4.
Dist from C2C: 300m. Pub 1km.
01900 85315
www.buttermerecumbria.com
CEdm85315@aol.com

Over Whinlatter

Directions

- The first real challenge comes when you leave High Lorton: the uphill slog to Whinlatter, the first section of which is unremitting, until you join the B5292 on the Whinlatter Pass.
- You should bear right along the forest track, then first left along the wide track, ignoring other routes to the right. This takes you over rough terrain for a couple of kilometres before coming out on the B5292, at which point go left then right for the Whinlatter Visitor Centre (if for any reason the off-road track is closed, as it was when I last cycled the C2C, continue along the road to the visitor centre).
- You are in the heart of England's only mountain forest. Because of the pure mountain air a sanatorium used to stand in the Whinlatter Forest. Sailors with TB and other communicable diseases were kept there in isolation. Beyond the visitor centre, pictured below, the route goes sharp right down a forest track to Thornthwaite, commanding some stunning views of Bassenthwaite Lake.
- Take time, weather permitting, to admire Blencathra, Skiddaw and, over to the right, Helvellyn.
- There is now an extensive range of mountain bike routes and Whinlatter is fast becoming the hub for northern Lakeland off-roading.
- Also leave yourself enough time to have a good look around the visitor centre. There's a wealth of forest habitat information, a fine tea room and shop.
  www.forestry.gov.uk/whinlatterhome
  017687 78469
- After Thornthwaite the route links up with the Workington to Keswick alternative, via Braithwaite and Portinscale, where there are some charming accommodation possibilities.

Our fully equipped workshop and shop is at the top of the first major challenge (climb) on your C2C. We can fix, fettle & check over any mechanical issue you may have on your bike. We also have a well stocked shop that supplies power gels, tubes or anything else you may have forgotten. Unfortunately we don't stock new legs! Alternatively , feel free to pop in for a chat, a free brew or directions.

whinlatter@cyclewisetraining.co.uk or tel: 017687 78711

Workington to Keswick

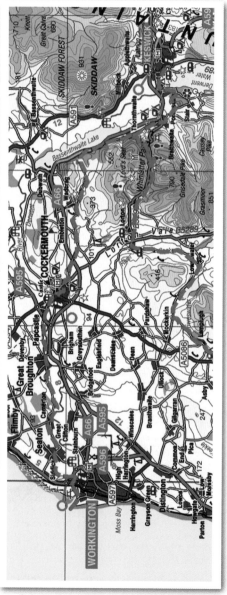

Ordnance Survey © Crown copyright: 100039985

Workington

Departure Route

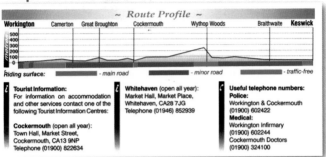

~ *Route Profile* ~

| Workington | Camerton | Great Broughton | Cockermouth | Wythop Woods | Braithwaite | **Keswick** |

Riding surface: — main road — minor road — traffic-free

i **Tourist Information:**
For information on accommodation and other services contact one of the following Tourist Information Centres:

Cockermouth (open all year):
Town Hall, Market Street,
Cockermouth, CA13 9NP
Telephone (01900) 822634

i **Whitehaven** (open all year):
Market Hall, Market Place,
Whitehaven, CA28 7JG
Telephone (01946) 852939

Useful telephone numbers:
Police:
Workington & Cockermouth
(01900) 602422
Medical:
Workington Infirmary
(01900) 602244
Cockermouth Doctors
(01900) 324100

Workington heading for Cockermouth

- The route starts from the lighthouse. You get there by turning down Curwen Road on the industrial estate. From the lighthouse turn left onto the railway bridge just by the sailing club, then (briefly) follow the path by the side of the river Derwent.
- Bear left at the next railway bridge, crossing the line at the road junction, where you turn right.
- At the main road go right and under the sandstone bridge where you meet the walkway/cycle path which then bears left, heading out of the industrial part of Workington past the lagoon and up through Seaton.
- Follow the route through Camerton, briefly joining the river again, skirting Broughton Moor and on through Great Broughton and Papcastle, once the site of a Roman fort. You are now on the edge of Cockermouth.

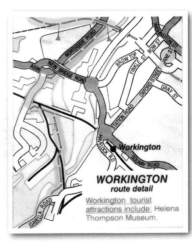

Workington

WORKINGTON
route detail

Workington tourist attractions include: Helena Thompson Museum.

31

About the town

European funding is being used to help restore this fine working town and there are high hopes that its resurgence will bring with it tourism and a new lease of life, as has happened in Whitehaven and Maryport further up the coast. Work on the town centre finished in 2007 after two years of mayhem and now there are new shops and a fine new silver municipal clock. There are some splendid examples of Georgian architecture and some powerful industrial heritage. Workington is an ancient market and industrial town at the mouth of the River Derwent.

Parts of it date back to Roman times but it was not until the 18th century, with the exploitation of local iron ore and coal, that Workington expanded to become a major industrial town and port.

In this respect its growth mirrors that of its neighbour, Whitehaven eight miles down the coast. Iron and steel manufacturing have always been part of Workington's *raison d'être*, and it was here that Henry Bessemer first introduced his revolutionary steel making process, florally commemorated in this picture.

In recent years, with the decline of the steel industry and coal mining, the town has had to diversify and with the refurbishment of the town centre it is ready to welcome tourists to its heart.

The advantage of starting here is that the opening leg of the journey is seven miles shorter, has gentler gradients and passes through the Georgian market town of Cockermouth. It is also close to, and goes through, Camerton, where the church sits prettily on the banks of the Derwent and the splendidly named Black Tom Inn beckons alluringly to passers-by.

It has some nice churches. The parish church of St Michael's has been on its present site since the 7th century, although the 12th century Norman church was replaced in 1770 by a larger building. Sadly this was severely damaged by fire in 1994, but has since undergone a major rebuilding programme. St John's Church was built in 1823 to commemorate the battle of Waterloo, to a design by Thomas Hardwick. It is built of local sandstone, and bears some resemblance to Inigo Jones's St Paul's Church in Covent Garden, London.

Workington Tourist Information Centre 01900 606699

Places of Interest

Workington Hall

Workington Hall is built around a pele tower dating from the 14th century, and was once one of the finest manor houses in the region.

This striking ruin, once owned by the Curwen family, Lords of the Manor of Workington, gave shelter to Mary Queen of Scots on her last flight from Scotland before her imprisonment and execution.

It is said to be haunted by Henry Curwen, who sunk the nearby Jane Pit in the 19th century, the remains of which can be seen at nearby Mossbay.

Town Museum

The Helena Thompson Museum was bequeathed to the people of Workington by the eponymous Miss Thompson, a local philanthropist, in 1940. It houses displays of pottery, silver, glass, and furniture dating from Georgian times, as well as the social and industrial history of Workington and the surrounding area.

Where to eat

Impressions, 173 Vulcans Lane. **01900 605 446**
Super Fish, 20 Pow Street Sit-in or takeaway. **01900 604 916**
Blue Dolphin, 1 Lismore Place Sit-in or t-away. **01900 604114**
Carnegie Colours Cafe, Finkle Street Home-cooking. **01900 605743**
Treats, 26 Finkle Street Good cafe. **01900 871752**
The Old Townhouse, Portland Square. Upmarket. **01900 871332**
Tarantella, 15-19 Wilson Street Good new Italian. **0871 5297487**

Cycle Shops

Bike Bank, 18-20 Market Place. **01900 603 337**
Halfords, Derwent Howe Retail Park. **01900 601 635**

Accommodation

Morven House Hotel, Siddick Rd, Workington, Cumbria CA14 1LE
Run by: Mrs Caroline Nelson
Right at the start of the C2C and close to the finish of the Reivers, the Morven is relaxed and well fit for purpose. All bedrooms are en-suite, comfortable. Large detached house with car park and secure cycle storage. You can leave your cars until you return if you wish.
Rooms: 2D, 6T (all en-suite)
B&B: £30-38
Pk Lunch: £4.50
Eve Meal: £10-£12
Distance from C2C: On route
VisitBritain 3 stars
01900 602118
www.morvenguesthouse.com
cnelsonmorven@aol.com

Armidale Cottages, 29 High Seaton, CA14 1PD
Run by: Susan and Fred Dahl
Just a few hundred yards from the track and five minutes from the start/finish, Armidale is set in half an acre of land with a small orchard. It has wood-burning stoves in the lounge and dining room and is centrally heated. There are slate floors in the lounge and hall with wood floors in the dining room and bedroom. Great breakfast and top end accommodation. Credit cards now accepted. Also handy for the Hadrian Way.
Rooms: 2D
B&B: £28-£35
Nr pub: The Coachman, 5 minutes walk
Pk Lunch: On request
Local inspection: Commended
01900 63704
www.armidalecottages.co.uk
armidalecotts@hotmail.com

Cockermouth

This is one of the most attractive towns in the northwest and is one of only two places in the Lake District to be designated a 'Gem Town' by the Department of the Environment 40 years ago. That means it is protected and will, in essence, remain the same in perpetuity.

It is just outside the boundary of the Lake District National Park and perhaps for this reason is not inundated with tourists and the tackiness that often goes with the industry.

It developed at the confluence of two great salmon rivers – the Cocker, which flows out of lakes Buttermere, Crummock and Loweswater; and the Derwent, which runs through lakes Derwent and Bassenthwaite to Workington.

The town got its market charter in 1221, and has retained its importance over the centuries. Later there was quarrying and mining for lead and iron outside the town, and a brewery at the foot of the castle mound, where the two rivers meet.

It has long fascinated writers, poets and artists and is the birthplace of William and Dorothy Wordsworth – one of the finest buildings here is Wordsworth House, pictured above, the Lakeland poet's family home, which is now in the care of the National Trust.

The great architectural guru Sir Nikolaus Pevsner, in his 'Buildings of England', described the place as 'quite a swagger house for such a town'. Built in 1745 for the then High Sheriff of Cumberland, Joshua Lucock, it was bought in 1761 by Sir James Lowther, son of Sir John, who built Whitehaven and its port. John Wordsworth, the poet's father, moved to Cockermouth as agent to Sir James in 1764, and in 1766 married and moved into the house. Here four sons and a daughter were born. Their mother died when William was eight, and he went to live with relations in Penrith.

The house thrived as a private residence until 1937, when it was put on the market. Since it was in a prime location in the centre of town, bosses of the local bus company snapped it up as the natural spot for a bus station. They applied for – and got – planning permission to bulldoze it, but there was such a national outcry that funds were raised for the town to buy it back and hand it over to the National Trust. The old kitchen and the housekeeper's room now serve as a café/restaurant where you can get morning coffee, light lunches and afternoon tea.

Two other famous men were born in Eaglesfield, a mile from the town's centre: Fletcher Christian, the man who led the mutiny on the Bounty was born in 1764, and attended the same school as Wordsworth; then in 1766 came John Dalton, a brilliant scientist and originator of atomic theory.

Cockermouth Castle was built in the 13th century, but not much of it remains because of the efforts of Robert the Bruce and his marauding Scots. Most of the remaining ruins are from a later period, between 1360 and 1370.

Places of Interest

Jennings Brewery
Offers 1½ hour tours around its premises, pictured below, explaining the processes involved in brewing traditional beer.
0845 1297185, www.jenningsbrewery.co.uk

The Museum of Printing
A fascinating range of printing presses brought together from all over Britain. 01900 824984

The Bitter End, 15 Kirkgate
The first pub in Cumbria with its own working brewery – 'Cumbria's Smallest Brewery'. 01900 828993
www.bitterend.co.uk.

Lakeland Sheep & Wool Centre
01900 822673
At the roundabout on the A66 is where you can meet Cumbria's most famous residents.

Castlegate House
Contemporary art exhibitions.
01900 822149

The Toy & Model Museum
Mainly British toys from 1900 onwards.
01900 827606

Tourist Information Centre
Town Hall, Market Place, Cockermouth, CA13 9NP
01900 822634

Where to eat

Beatfords CountryRestaurant, 7 Lowther Went. **01900 827099**
Cheers Bistro, 22, Main St. **01900 822109**
The Bitter End Brew Pub, 15 Kirkgate
Excellent value, great beer and
great food. **01900 828993**
Junipers Restaurant & Cafe Bar,
11 South St. **01900 822892**
Quince & Medlar, 13 Castlegate. Fine
food – vegetarian. **01900 823579**
Norham Coffee House & Restaurant,
73 Main St **01900 824330**
Oscar's Bistro, 18-20 Market
Place. **01900 823654**
Nikki's Italian Restaurant &
Bistro, 7 Old Kings Arms Lane.
01900 821223
Taste of India, 4-5 Headford Court,
Main Street. **01900 827844**
Lee's Chinese Takeaway and Fish &
Chips, 47 Main St. **01900 827770**

Accommodation

Rose Cottage, Lorton Road, Cockermouth, Cumbria CA13 9DX
Run by: John and Susan Graham
A family run guest house in its own grounds. All rooms en-
suite with colour TV, tea/coffee, central heating and all are now
double glazed. Warm friendly atmosphere.
Rooms: 4D, 3T, 2F, 1S
B&B: £32.50–£45
Pk Lunch: from £6.50
Eve Meal: £22 for 3 courses
Dist from C2C: 400m
Pubs nearby
01900 822189
www.rosecottageguest.co.uk
bookings@rosecottageguest.co.uk

Allerdale Court Hotel, Market Place, CA13 9NQ

Run by: John Carlin

Warm hospitality, good food, comfort and dedicated attention to detail is what this family run establishment prides itself on. Cosy yet fashionable, the Allerdale welcomes cyclists, golfers and general holidaymakers with equal courtesy.

Rooms: 5T, 4S, 12D/S

B&B: £44-£72

Eve meal: Pickwick: £17.95 2-courses; £21.95 3-courses. Oscars Bistro: £5.95-£13.95

Pk lunch: By arrangement

01900 823654

www.allerdalecourthotel.co.uk

info@allerdalecourthotel.co.uk

Orchard House, Embleton, Cockermouth, Cumbria, CA13 9XP

Run by: Barbara Newton

Orchard House is a lovely detached Edwardian house set within 0.75 acres of garden. We are a small and friendly establishment and will welcome you with tea and cake. We serve a delicious breakfast to set you on your way.

Rooms: 3D, 1T (prior notice for twin)

B&B: £27 1st night & £25. £30 single occupancy of double room.

Pk Lunch: from £5

Secure cycle parking, open all year excluding Christmas.

Dist from Route: 0.5 mile

Pub: 0.25 miles away

01900 822189

www.rosecottageguest.co.uk

bookings@rosecottageguest.co.uk

Riverside, 12 Market St, Cockermouth, Cumbria, CA13 9NJ

Run by: Rachel & Jean Habgood

Georgian home with comfortable beds, excellent breakfasts, local amenities, tea-trays and drying facilities plus bike lock-up. Next door to the Tourist Information Centre. Welcome!

Rooms: 2T, 1S

B&B: £23-25

Pk Lunch: £3.50 (prior notice, please)

Dist from Route: Right on C2C & Reivers

Pub: 0.25 miles away

01900 827504

Thornthwaite

Directions
Leaving Cockermouth and on to Thornthwaite

- Cross over Gote Street from the Papcastle road and continue past the James Walker factory, then right onto Bridge Street, crossing the river just after the doctor's surgery.
- You then head left onto Main Street. Go past Station Street before turning right into Challoner Street, left into Cocker Lane and then almost immediately right to follow the river. Go under Lorton Street towards the Youth Hostel, turn right to swivel over the River Cocker and follow the path past the cemetery before the hairpin right turn onto Strawberry Home Road, where you take a left. It is now a straightforward run.

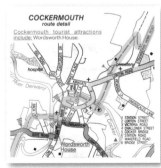

- You may wish to stop near the shores of Bassenthwaite's northern tip, in which case go through the village of Wythop Mill and turn right by the phone box.
- Turn left at the Pheasant Inn and go over the A66 onto the B5291,

taking the scenic Ouse Bridge to the Castle Hotel. After that, it's a short hop along the road and up to the village and the Sun Inn, where they serve good food and ale.

Assuming you do not opt for this diversion, you will encounter a short, hilly section before the descent to Bassenthwaite Lake, from whence it is an easy ride into Keswick. At Thornthwaite you meet up with the Whitehaven route.

Legend of Barf and the bishop

There is a Viking burial ground here at Powter Howe and just behind it is a hill called Barf.

You will see two large white rocks – one halfway up Barf, one at the bottom. The higher one is the Bishop, and the lower the Clerk. They commemorate the tale of a deadly 18th century drinking session at the Swan Inn (now transformed into holiday apartments) during which the bibulous Bishop of Londonderry (doubtless on diocesan duty) bet his clerk that he could beat him to the top of Barf. They downed their glasses and set off. The Right Reverend keeled over half-way up, while the clerk pegged it at the bottom. The stones are said to commemorate this foolhardy wager. I do not know whether they were on their way up or down. Informed readers are welcome to write in.

Thornthwaite overlooks Bassenthwaite Lake, the only lake in the Lake District. This may seem strange, but all the other expanses of H2O in the so-called Lake District are Waters, Meres or Tarns.

Accommodation

Lanefoot farm, Thornwaite, Nr Keswick, CA12 5RZ

Run by: Helen and Gareth Davies
Charming and informal campsite bang on the route with good facilities at good prices. There are a couple of fields, plenty of space and a proper country feel, within easy striking distance of pubs and restaurants.
017687 78097
www.stayinthornthwaite.co.uk
helen@stayinthornthwaite.co.uk

Powter Howe, Thornthwaite, Braithwaite, nr Keswick, CA12 5SQ

Run by: Keren Lockwood
Beautiful 16th century farmhouse of great character and magnificent views over Bassenthwaite Lake towards Skiddaw. Set in two acres of mature garden, once visited never forgotten!
Rooms: 2D, 1T, 1S.
B&B: £25.
Evening meal: Pub 2 miles.
Pk lunch: by arrangement.
017687 78415

Braithwaite

Directions
Merging the routes from all the starting points

- Nestling at the bottom of the Whinlatter Pass and Newlands Valley with the spectacular backdrop of Grisedale Pike and Bassenthwaite Lake, the routes from Whitehaven / St Bees & Egremont and from Workington merge in time to take you to the picturesque village of Braithwaite.
- Braithwaite is half way between Thornthwaite and Keswick. It's an excellent base for touring the Lake District, close to Loweswater, Crummock Water and Buttermere.
- It's a straight and pleasant run through a quintessentially English village scene, over a Medieval humped-back bridge. This section of Braithwaite, leading out towards Little Braithwaite and Ullock, is somehow preserved in time. Only cars spoil the scene – otherwise you could be back in the 18th century.

Cycle Repairs
Ian Hindmarch fixes bikes in his workshop next to the village stores , next to the hump-back bridge.
017687 78273.

Accommodation

Scotgate Holiday Park, Briathwaite, Keswick, CA12 5TF
Scotgate Chalet, Camping & Caravan Park near Keswick is an outstanding holiday centre on the threshold of the Lake District's most popular scenery. Superbly placed between Derwentwater and Bassenthwaite Lake, with dramatic views towards Skiddaw and the northern fells, it makes the perfect base for exploring by bike, whether you are just spending one night or taking a little more time over it.
Coffee Shop, Braithwaite village: 500m
Shower rooms, laundry
Licensed Shop.
Chalet rentals by arrangement
017687 78343
scotgateholidaypark.co.uk
info@scotgateholidaypark.co.uk

The Coledale Inn, Braithwaite, Nr Keswick, Cumbria CA12 5TN

Run By: Geoff and Charley Mawdsley

The Coledale is a genuine country inn situated above Braithwaite Village in a peaceful hillside position well away from passing traffic. It is ideal for cycling and walking, with paths to the mountains immediately outside the hotel gardens. Ideal spot to explore the area for those not in a rush.

Rooms: 2S, 11D, 6T, 1F
B&B: £37.
Evening meal: £8.50-£12.50.
Pk lunch: £4.50.
On route, VisitBritain 3-stars.
017687 78272
www.coledale-inn.co.uk
info@coledale-inn.co.uk

Keswick

Directions
Braithwaite to Keswick

- The route to Keswick via Portinscale is well signposted. You come into the town up the main street, following the traffic to the left and up to the lights at the Penrith Road. If not stopping in this delightful town, then go left down Station Street, turn right onto Brundholme Road, round in a loop and pick up the track heading east.

Sandwiched between Derwentwater, Blencathra and Skiddaw at the entrance to the mighty Borrowdale valley, this market town is blessed with one of Britain's most idyllic settings.
It is ideal for cycling, walking, boating or just sightseeing, and is a favourite venue with cycle back-up teams; it is the most popular and best-equipped stop-off point on the route.
Keswick ('Cese-Wic' - the Cheese Town, literally) became

prosperous in the 17th century, during the reign of Elizabeth I, thanks to copper, lead, silver and iron mining.

There was so much work that engineers had to be imported from Germany. Despite a rocky start – at one stage, local xenophobia drove them to inhabit Derwent Island – they soon managed to integrate; evidence of this can be found in the phone book today, with its many Germanic surnames.

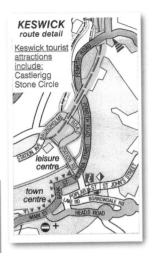

KESWICK route detail

Keswick tourist attractions include: Castlerigg Stone Circle

Lead in your pencils...

The town's Cumberland Pencil Company was established after the discovery of graphite in Borrowdale in the 16th century. However, the town was granted its charter some 300 years before that by Edward I in 1276. Visitors started to flock in during the 18th century and Victorian times. Many of them were literary pilgrims, attracted by the association with such Romantic poets as Southey, Coleridge and Wordsworth. John Ruskin, the aesthete and champion of the Pre-Raphaelites, had close associations with the town.

The population of the place has grown little in the past century. In 1902 there were 4,500 people; now there are just 500 more, but many of them – as you will note if you choose to stop over – are B&B owners. The place also has many good pubs and solid restaurants.

Cycle Shops

Chris Warren, Kinniside, Portinscale, **01768 72415**

Keswick Moutain Bike Centre (Hire/Servicing) Unit 1, Daleston Court, Southey Hill, Keswick **01768 775202**

Keswick Riding & Cycle Hire Centre, hire & minor spares/repairs.

Places of Interest

The Cumberland Pencil Museum, West of the town centre. **017687 73626**

Cars of the Stars, this is a pre-Carbon Footprint establishment. Famous cars including a James Bondmobile, the Batmobile and Chitty Chitty Bang Bang. **017687 73757**

The Keswick Launch Company, tours on the lake, on the shore of Derwentwater. **017687 72263**.

43

George Fisher, big stock of outdoor gear, books and maps. Borrowdale Rd. 017687 72178

Cotswold Outdoor Ltd, as above. 017687 81939

The Moot Hall, Tourist Information Centre. 017687 72645

Theatre by the Lake, Lakeside. Open all year round. Restaurant. Beautiful setting. 017687 74411

Alhambra Cinema, St.Johns St. 017687 72195
Castlerigg Stone Circle, thought to date from 3000 B.C. Steep climb out of town on the alternative Penrith Rd route. Worth detour.

Keswick Museum & Art Gallery, interesting and eclectic collection 017687 72263

Where to eat

Lemon & Lime, 31 Lake Road. International cuisine with tapas, pizzas and other family favourites: **017687 73088**

Salsa Mexican Bistro, 1 New Street. Spicy and popular medium priced establishment owned by the Nellist brothers: **017687 75222**

Red Fort Indian Restaurant, 5 St John Street. Lively and reliable spot very popular with the locals: **017687 74328**

Swinside Inn, Newlands, Keswick 017687 78253

Luca's Ristorante, High Hill, Greta Bridge. Family run Italian with elaborate decorations and prices to match: **017687 74621**

Maysons Restaurant and Cafe, 33, Lake Road, Keswick, simple and unpretentious eaterie. Good value: **017687 74104**

The Bank Tavern, 47 Main St. Solid, handsome pub with good, traditional English cooking. Medium price. Outside eating area: **017687 72663**

George Hotel, 3 St John St. Medium priced fare: **017687 75751**

The Lakeland Pedlar, Wholefood Cafe and Bicycle Centre, Bell Close, Keswick, CA12 5JD. Great food, drink and bike accessories, all under the same roof. 017687 74492, www.LakelandPedlar.co.uk

Accommodation

Powe House, Portinscale, Keswick, Cumbria CA12 5RW
Run by: Andrew & Helen Carey
Elegant Georgian house recently and lovingly restored.
Bedrooms fully en-suite with LCD screens. All food is locally
sourced and there is a solid and secure bike lock-up.
Rooms: 5D (3 of which can become twins) plus 1S
B&B: from £32.
Pk lunch: from £4.
VisitBritain: 4-stars Silver Award.
On route.
017687 73611
www.powehouse.com
andrewandhelen@powehouse.com

The Mount, Portinscale, Keswick, Cumbria CA12 5RD
Run by: Tony Mannion
Friendly, family run
and comfortable B&B in quiet setting. En-suite
rooms. Splendid lake/fell views. Excellent breakfasts
with vegetarian option. The Mount has been a firm cyclists'
favourite for more than a decade.
Rooms: 1S,3D,1T.
B&B: £34.
Pk lunch: £6.
Distance from C2C: on route.
Pub: 200m.
Secure cycle storage.
017687 73970
www.mountkeswick.co.uk
mount.keswick@btinternet.com

Denton House, Penrith Rd, Keswick, CA12 4JW
Run by: Rebecca Chaffer
Budget accommodation run by Cedric and Rebecca. This is a
big, friendly outdoor hostel, full of youngsters and the not so
young. Lots of fun and cheerful. Group bookings welcome by
arrangement. Inside storage for bikes.
Rooms: 8 containing 58 bunk beds.
B&B: £13 during week. £14 weekends. Breakfast for groups of
10 or more: £3.
Pk lunch: £5 (groups only).
Evening meal: from £5 (groups only).
Pub: 200m.
On route.
01768 775351
www.vividevents.co.uk
sales@vividevents.co.uk

Beckside, 5 Wordsworth St, Keswick, CA12 4HU

Run by: Tracey and Andrew Graham
Taken over by Tracy and Andrew a couple of years ago, the fine cycling traditions have been maintained right down to the killer

breakfast (optional). The parting fry-up has been described as all-embracing - you will soon be murdering these calories. Rooms en-suite, secure bike storage.
Rooms: 2D, 1T/F.
B&B: £30.
Pk lunch: on request - prior notice, please.
VisitBritain: 4-stars
017687 73093
www.beckside–keswick.co.uk
info@beckside–keswick.co.uk

Springs Farm, Springs Rd, Keswick, CA12 4AN

Run by: Hazel Hutton
Comfortable accommodation in a large 19th century farmhouse at the foot of Walla Crag. This is a working dairy farm offering quality accommodation in an idyllic location. It is a 10 minute walk into town. This has been home to the Hutton family since 1924 and remains an entirely family operated business to this day. There is a pretty courtyard with ample parking. To the rear is a large orchard with apple, pear and plum trees, where free-range hens lay your breakfast eggs. And now there's a satellite TV, too. There are also 2 cottages sleeping 6 & 2 available for rent.
Rooms: 2D, 1T.
B&B: £34-£36.
Nearest pub: 1 mile to town centre.
VisitBritain: 3 stars.
017687 72144/07816 824253
www.springsfarmcumbria.co.uk
info@springsfarmcumbria.co.uk

Twa Dogs Inn, Penrith Rd, Keswick, CA12 4JU

Run by: Peter & Marjorie Harding
Traditional family run concern with an atmosphere as warm as the welcome. Open fires, dominoes, darts & pool in a proper pub. Lock-up for bikes and a range of real ales for their owners.

Rooms: 1T, 1F (3S & 1D), 3D. (E-S).
B&B: £30pp. Kids negotiable.
EM: from £6.95.
Pk lunch: £5.
Distance from C2C: just above the railway line coming out of Keswick.
017687 72599
www.twadogs.co.uk

The Queens Hotel, Main St, Keswick, CA12 5JF

Right in the centre of town on the market square, and a hub of the action since being rebuilt in 1826, the Queens offers high standards of comfort and service and has 35 en-suite guest rooms. There is a secure lock-up for bikes and everything a tired cyclist could need. Recently and stylishly refurbished, there is an open fire in the bar.

Rooms: 5S, 12T/F, 18D
B&B: from £40. Special deals available.
Evening meal: main courses £6-£8.
Pk lunch: by arrangement.
01768 773333
www.queenshotel.co.uk
info@queenshotel.co.uk

Honister House, 1 Borrowdale RD, Keswick, CA12 5DD

Run by: John & Susie Stakes
"A warm welcome awaits you at our 18th century home in the centre of Keswick. Cyclists, walkers and families welcome. Drying room and storage. Award-winning breakfasts. Vegetarian options. Brochure available. One night occupation often available."

Rooms: 1D, 1T, 1F.
B&B: £35 - £37.50.
Pk lunch: £4.
AA 4-stars & AA Breakfast Award.
Pub: 1 minute.
017687 73181
www.honisterhouse.co.uk
honisterhouse@btconnect.com

Cranford House, 18 Eskin St, Keswick, CA12 4DG

Run by: Carol Hallgarth
Tasteful, doily-free, cycle friendly and comfortable stop-off. Just a couple of minutes from the town centre. Drying facilities and secure storage.

Rooms: 2S, 3T/D,1D.
B&B: £27-£30.
Pk lunch: £4.
017687 71017
www.cranfordhouse.co.uk
carolcranfordhouse@tiscali.co.uk

Ordnance Survey © Crown copyright: 100039985

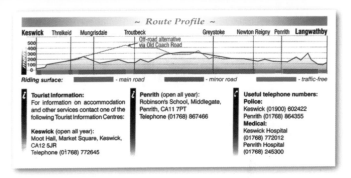

~ Route Profile ~

| Keswick | Threlkeld | Mungrisdale | Troutbeck | Greystoke | Newton Reigny | Penrith | Langwathby |

Off-road alternative via Old Coach Road

500 400 300 200 100 0

Riding surface: ▬▬ - main road ▬▬ - minor road ▬▬ - traffic-free

Tourist Information:
For information on accommodation and other services contact one of the following Tourist Information Centres:

Keswick (open all year):
Moot Hall, Market Square, Keswick, CA12 5JR
Telephone (01768) 772645

Penrith (open all year):
Robinson's School, Middlegate, Penrith, CA11 7PT
Telephone (01768) 867466

Useful telephone numbers:
Police:
Keswick (01900) 602422
Penrith (01768) 864355
Medical:
Keswick Hospital
(01768) 772012
Penrith Hospital
(01768) 245300

Directions and route choices

- There are two ways out of Keswick. The most popular – and by far the easier – is the one that follows the old Keswick-Penrith railway line and the river Greta as far as Threlkeld. It is a beautiful and leafy stretch. You get to it down Station Road and Brundholme Road, bearing left at the swimming pool and heading in front of the old station.
- The alternative takes you up into the hills above the town, but is only for the fit and even then watch the weather reports before taking to the upper slopes.
- Both routes assume the same start, unless you want to go out of Keswick along the old Penrith road.

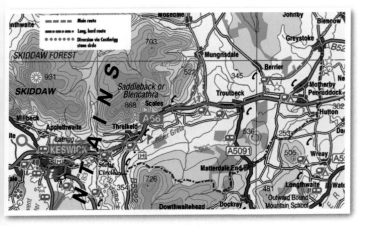

Up hill and up dale

If you're feeling energetic and (seriously) fit, try the Old Coach Road over the hills. It branches from the railway route, just before the track goes under the A66 viaduct, and goes up the steep slope to Castlerigg Stone Circle. Press on through St John's in the Vale, Matterdale End and down to Greystoke via Hutton John.

The Coach Road (what coach could possibly have tackled this?) is a seriously rough off-road alternative and very exposed. Check the weather before tackling it and don't do it if you're not certain of your capabilities.

There is accommodation where the route crosses the A5091 at Matterdale (see Troutbeck, and further along, just off the A66, Penruddock & Motherby) before the route rejoins the alternative at Greystoke.

The middle way

Start along the toughest route described above but after stopping to admire the Castlerigg circle, bear left down the hill and rejoin the more sedate option.

The main route

This takes you fairly effortlessly alongside the River Greta, all the way to Threlkeld.

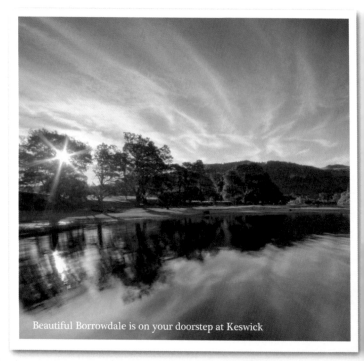

Beautiful Borrowdale is on your doorstep at Keswick

Threlkeld & Scales

About Threlkeld

History from hunting to mining and back

Blencathra, known locally as Saddleback, overlooks this
traditional and pretty village. There are also views towards
Clough Head and the Helvellyn range.

Threlkeld is, I gather, Norse for 'the spring of the thrall' – thrall
being a bonded servant. Zinc, lead and granite were mined
during the last century until the last of the granite miners hung
up their shovels and picks in the mid-80s.

At one time more than a hundred men were employed in the
mines and at the quarry there is a museum with an impressive
mineral collection, mining artefacts and touching reminders of
how things used to be.

A table top relief map of the Lake District and a pictorial
history of Threlkeld are also on display. There was once a TB
isolation hospital which is now a field centre for biologists and
geographers.

Since the Dark Ages and the days of Sir Lancelot de Threlkeld,
hunting has been an integral part of local life; this is the home of
the Blencathra Hunt, the Lakeland pack that traditionally hunts
on foot rather than on horseback and claims that its dogs are
descended from those used by John Peel of song fame.

The Threlkeld sheepdog trials are a highlight of the year and
feature foxhound and terrier shows, as well as hound training.

All of these rural pursuits are, one presumes, finding life tougher
these days.

Accommodation

Horse & Farrier Inn, Threlkeld, nr Keswick, CA12 4SQ
Run by: Ian Court & Susan Whalley
The Horse & Farrier enjoys an idyllic location in the centre of the picturesque village of Threlkeld, just four miles east of Keswick. Built in 1688 at the foot of Blencathra, with stunning views. 'Cask Marque' Real Ales and extensive wine list are served in the bar, restaurant or beer garden. Excellent reputation for good food, using seasonal local produce always freshly prepared. Numerous reccommendations include an AA two rosette accreditation. AA listed, AA Hotel, Restaurant & Pub Guides
Rooms: 2S, 6D, 1T.
B&B: £40.
Evening meal:£6.95-£15.
Pk lunch: £6.
017687 79688
www.horseandfarrier.com
enquiries@horseandfarrier.com

Horse & Farrier Guest House, Threlkeld, nr Keswick, CA12 4SQ
Run by: Ian Court & Susan Whalley
The Horse & Farrier Guest House is opposite the pub's rear car park just a few seconds walk from the Inn and offers an additional four rooms. All the main services are offered in the Inn, such as breakfast, lunch and dinner. All the Horse & Farrier special offers apply to the guest house and all rooms offer tea & coffee making facilities, TV / DVD and hair dryers. There is a television lounge with DVD, reading books and a selection of board games. Additional facilities include: ironing board, drying room, bike lock up and newspapers. Large parties wishing to hire the facility for more than five days will get special rates.
Rooms: 3T/D, 1D.
B&B: £40.
Eve meal (at pub): £6.95-£15.
Pk lunch: £6.
017687 79688
www.horseandfarrier.com
enquiries@horseandfarrier.com

The Hollies, Threlkeld, nr Keswick, CA12 4RX

John & Margaret Fleet

Fine stone-built house with spectacular views to front and rear. John & Margaret have been in the hotel business for 30 years so know how to look after you. Ample parking. Great breakfast. Bathrooms recently refurbished plus new de-luxe room for those wishing to pamper themselves after a hard day's ride.

AA 4 diamonds.
Rooms: 4T/D.
B&B: £35-£40.
Pk lunch £4.
Eve Meal: Horse & Farrier.
017687 79216 or 07887 611127
www.theholliesinlakeland.co.uk
info@theholliesinlakeland.co.uk

Next Stop Scales

After Threlkeld there is a short section along a car-free country road, then a cycle path alongside the A66 until **Scales**, before you go along a delightful gated lane to Mungrisdale. Don't forget to look up to admire Blencathra on your left and the Helvellyn range to the right.

Scales Farm Country Guest House, Threlkeld, CA12 4SY

Run by: Alan & Angela Jameison
Modernised 17th century Lakeland farmhouse at the foot of Blencathra overlooking the northern Lake District fells. Trad & vegetarian breakfasts. Immaculate throughout.
Rooms: 3D, 1F, 2T/D en-suite.
B&B: £33-£38.
Evening meal: pub next door.
Pk lunch: £4.50-£6.
VisitBritain: 4 stars Silver Award.
017687 79660
www.scalesfarm.com
scales@scalesfarm.com

Mungrisdale/Troutbeck

The village of Mungrisdale comprises a traditional inn, a church and a cluster of houses huddled around the river Glenderamackin. The inn is changing hands in July 2009 and we await reports. A truly restful spot, you reach it along the gated road from which there are spectacular views of the fells. Souther and Blencathra lie to the West and the Ullswater fells to the South whilst to the east the daunting prospect of the Pennines loom imposingly.

- The Sustrans route suggests you cross the river just short of the village, but that would be a shame. There is an alternative exit path over minor lanes, through Berrier and onto the Greystoke road, or follow the lane back down the other side of the Glenderamackin to the A66, where the cycle path takes over.

- At the top of the hill you can follow the route to the left or carry straight on for Greystoke. Either will do.

- Troutbeck is about two miles further along the A66 once you have returned to it from Mungrisdale.

- Be very careful crossing, though. Many a motorist attempts the land speed record on this stretch.

Motherby & Penruddock

Accommodation

Herdwick Inn, Penruddock, CA11 0QU.
Run by: Linda & Mark Wilmot
Traditional 18th century country inn with
log fire offering good home cooked food
made from local ingredients. Great duck
and lamb, local pies. Warm welcome
and some fine real ales. Rooms recently
refurbished. Sunday carvery is very
popular. On the B5288 to Greystoke,
the alternative route via Motherby, and
increasingly popular with cyclists. All
rooms now have en-suite facilities.
Rooms: 1T, 3D, 1S.
B&B: £35-£45.
Evening meal: £7.77-£13.95.
Pk lunch: from £4 (notice preferred).
VisitBritain: 4 stars.
01768 483007
www.herdwickinn.com
info@herdwickinn.com

For the Camper
Beckses Caravan Park
Penruddock, CA11 0RX.
Run by: Teasdale Family
Pleasant little spot right
on the route. Ideal for
those wishing to hire a
caravan for a few days or
merely wishing to pitch
camp for the night.
01768 83224

Motherby House, Motherby, nr Penrith, Cumbria CA11 0RJ

Run by: Jacquie Freeborn
Warm, friendly former 18th century farmhouse. Excellent food for outdoor appetites and muddy clothes welcome. Jacquie can take groups of up to 12.
Rooms: 2F.
B&B: £25.50.
Evening meal :£16 3-courses.
Pk lunch: £6.50.
Nearest pub: 1 mile.
017684 83368
motherbyhouse.co.uk
jacquie@motherbyhouse.co.uk

Trentham House, Motherby, Penrith, Cumbria CA11 0RJ

Run by: Mo & Spen Glover
This attractive room is light and spacious with extensive views from its picture window. The private facilities are of a high standard. The C2C (B5288) passes the driveway and cycle storage is lockable. Ideal for couples.
Rooms: 1D with private facilities.
B&B: £27.50
Secure cycle storage. Drying facilities.
On route. Pubs within the mile.
017684 83459 or 07771 985011
www.trenthamhouse.homestead.com
spencerglover06@aol.com

Greystoke

About the village
Paying homage to the original Tarzan

This traditional English village, 8km west of Penrith, was built around a green with a pub and a church the size of a cathedral. Discreetly hidden at the top of a long drive and behind a curtain of trees in a 3,000-acre wooded park is Greystoke Castle, seat of the Howard family since the 1500s when they were emerging as movers and shakers behind the monarchies of the late Tudors and early Stuarts.

Tarzan is modelled on one former Baron Greystoke, and there are certainly enough trees for any Lord of the Apes to practice on. It is a family home and business rather than a theme park, so not much is made of the Tarzan link, but I thought Tarzan fans might be interested.

The village is probably Roman in origin, lying alongside the road they built from Penrith to Troutbeck. The name means 'place by the River Creik', a small stream nearby. The village was known as Creistock in early Medieval times.

Though most of the village dates from the 17th century, the foundation of the Perpendicular-style church was laid in the mid-1200s, though building did not start until 1382 and went on into the next century. The bells that still ring out in Greystoke date from the Middle Ages. Inside is some fine Medieval and Victorian stained glass (see picture).

The Spillers Stone in the village was thought to be a plague stone, where plague victims left coins in a pool of vinegar on its concave surface. The vinegar was supposed to protect the healthy, who left food there for sufferers. According to the Cumbria Directory, Greystoke Castle was an integral part of village life, the first version being constructed in 1129 as protection against Scottish Border raiders, early versions of the Reivers, that came to dominate the area before the cycle route picked up the nomenclature.

Cromwell destroyed much of Greystoke and a devastating fire in 1868 ensured that only the medieval pele (fortified) tower and a few Georgian interiors survived and the present building, though it mimics the Elizabethan style, actually dates from the 19th century. The nearby countryside boasts a number of fine old fortified houses complete with pele towers, notably Blencowe Hall, built in 1590, Greenthwaite Hall, and Johnby Hall. All are reminders of the bloody times in the Borders.

The Boot and Shoe pub in the village acquired its name because of the strange sartorial habit of a former Duke of Norfolk of wearing a shoe on one foot and a boot on the other, to ease the pain of crippling gout. Whether or not, thus clad, he shuffled down the long drive and across the green to the pub is not recorded.

He would have done better settling for tea and scones at Annie Swarbrick's Greystoke Cycle Cafe (see entry), a welcome addition to the village.

At time of going to press proposals were afoot to build nine 100m high wind turbines above the village - plans which are being fiercely opposed as they will have serious visual impact on this majestic spot. Those wishing to object should go to **www.blencathra.net.**

Accommodation

Brathen, The Thorpe, Greystoke, nr Penrith, Cumbria CA11 0TJ

Run by: Christine Mole

Distance from C2C: on route. Pub 300 yds

Comfortable barn conversion on the outskirts of the village with a warm welcome and hearty breakfasts using local produce.

Rooms: 2D, 2T, 2F.
B&B: £25-£30.
Pk lunch: £4.
01768483595
www.brathen.co.uk
stay@brathen.co.uk

Stafford House, Greystoke Castle, Greystoke

Run by: Hazel Knight

Large Victorian folly that looks like a walled Gothic castle within the grounds of Tarzan's castle (Greystoke) and shares the same magnificent drive. The house is Grade II listed and sits in nearly an an acre of its own grounds with castle battlements on three sides and arched windows. Aside from looking Medieval, it is very comfortable.

Rooms: 2D, 1T.
B&B: £35-£40.
Pk lunch: from £5.
Pub: half an arrow flight.
01768483558
07759133281
hazel.knight@btconnect.com

The Bunkhouse, Stafford House, Greystoke Castle, Greystoke,

Run by: Hazel Knight

This new bunkhouse sleeps up to 15 in two dormitories, Blencathra Lodge and Pennine Lodge. The head gardener for Greystoke Castle used to reside in the main house at this property and used the lodge to store all the home-grown fruit and supplies for the Howard family through the long winters. It is now fully kitted out with a fitted kitchen-diner, with every convenience including linen and towels, wet rooms & drying rooms. Lockers are available and one of the toilets is easily accessible for the disabled. Tea, coffee, fruit juice, various cereals, bread butter and jams and milk are provided. The rest can be found at the local shop which is only 5 minutes walk and offers a good choice of fare, the Boot & Shoe pub or the Cycle Cafe.

Location: grounds of Greystoke Castle, next to Stafford House

Saddleback dorm: sleeps 4-6 Blencathra dorm: sleeps 8-10

1 double room £20- (£30 for single occupancy).

Bunk House: £18.

Distance from pub: 400 yards.

Packed lunch: £5. Breakfast: £7.

017684 83558

07759 133281

hazel.knight@btconnect.com

Boot & Shoe, Greystoke, Penrith, CA11 0TP

Run by: Jan & Ben Mandale

Since Jan and Ben took over in July 07 the Boot & Shoe has enjoyed a new lease of life. There's a real buzz about the place; cyclists, jockeys and locals jostle for place while Jan hands out steaming plates of excellent food ranging from chicken balti to local dishes like Lamb Henry. A real community hub. Log fire in the bar, stove in the lounge plus selection of well kept real ales.

Rooms: 4T+1D/T (en-suite).

B&B: £30-£37.50.

Evening meal: £5.95-£12.95 (main courses).

Packed lunch: price depends on order.

017684 83343

www.boot-and-shoe.com

mandale@lineone.net

Greystoke Cycle Cafe, CA11 0UT
Run by: Annie Swarbrick
This is a splendid little stop off for a nice summer's day, or take shelter in the barn if it's not so nice. Annie's garden is a lovely spot and the home baked cakes, scones, paninis, bacon butties and home made soups are a treat. Tea, coffee, cold drinks and all the essentials you could imagine at this delightful pitstop just a stone's throw from the village green. Annie organises all sorts of activities from this old farmhouse - just take a look at 'Quirky Workshops' on the website. The Cyclists' Barn is open 10–6pm with hot drinks /cakes solely for those on bicycles. Great views across parkland to Greystoke Castle. Car/van parking for C2C support drivers only.

017684 83984
www.greystokecyclecafe.co.uk
annie@greystokecyclecafe.co.uk

Blencow Village

Accommodation

Little Blencowe Farm, Blencow, Penrith, Cumbria CA11 0DG
Run by: Barbara Fawcett

This 18th century farmhouse is comfortable and friendly and all rooms are furnished in keeping with period. The bedrooms have some aded luxuries, however, such as hospitality trays, hairdryers, TV and armchairs. Good wholesome breakfasts are provided using local produce and homemade bread and jams. An extensive evening meal menu is available on request, to be ordered in advance (there is also a good local pub which serves excellent food). Little Blencowe Farm is a mixed dairy and sheep farm with the milking of 150 Ayrshire cows being the main enterprise.

Rooms: 1T/D, 1D.
B&B: £27-£35.
Evening meal: please give notice.
£12 two courses; £15 for three.
Packed Lunch
Pub on doorstep
Secure lock up, on C2C route
01768 483338 or 07745 460186
www.littleblencowe.co.uk
bef@littleblencowe.wanadoo.co.uk

Blencowe Hall, Blencow, near Penrith, Cumbria, CA11 0DF

This Grade I twelve bedroom, 11 bath fortified manor with two pele towers works best for large groups who plan to spend some time in the local area (min stay is 3 nights). If there are 24 of you then it works out about the same price as a B&B. Anyone who has cycled the C2C will have seen this recently renovated building overlooking the Greystoke to Blencow lane. The courtyard entrance is dated 1590, but this is one of the newer bits. It has its own chapel and many genuine medieval features, such as spiral stone staircases and

inglenook fireplaces, all restored under the supervision of English Heritage. Massive welcome hamper including wine & breakfast items, T/D & W/M, 2 TVs. ***** rating from VisitBritain. Blencowe is rented out through Rural Retreats. See the website to get a fuller flavour.
Rooms 12. There are 11 bathrooms.
Rate £25-£50 a night depending on season (but don't forget that you need to fill the place).
Ample Parking / No dogs.
Aga kitchen. Medieval walls with 21st century comforts.
24 bicycles available for guest use (small charge).
Secure lock up.
Drying room linen & towels etc provided.
Fishing beat on the adjoining River Petteril.
30 acres of fields and gardens.
info@ruralretreats.co.uk
https:www.ruralretreats.co.uk/rr/properties/property.jsf?ref=CU037

Mill Farm, Blencow, Penrith, Cumbria CA11 0DF

Run by: Susan & Terry Foster
Delightful stone-built 18th-c farmhouse once part of the Greystoke estate. A sweeping gravel drive leads up to two ponds while terraces and patios surround the house. Magnificent views towards Ullswater and east over the Pennines. Early starts catered for with generous continental breakfasts. Susan runs a pony trekking centre at Ullswater for those wishing to switch saddles.
Rooms: 1D, 1F.
B&B: £25 (£30 for single occ).
Eve meal: The Crown in nearby village.
Pub on doorstep.
Secure lock up, on C2C route.
01768 4 83916 or
07764 304884

Penrith

Directions

Leaving Greystoke, then on to Newton Reigny and Penrith

- You soon pass Blencowe Hall (see p61), the aforementioned fortified farmhouse. It is an unusually handsome building just before you get to the village of Little Blencow. Just up the road follow signs to the right and you will enter Penrith via Newton Reigny and Newton Rigg.
- On leaving Newton Rigg campus go underneath the M6 and turn right at the T-junction, going into town along Robinson Street, across Scotland Rd and into Drover's Lane.
- The route is well sign-posted. You know you are on the right tracks when you find yourself exiting Penrith up Fell Lane – a steep climb to a T-junction at the top.

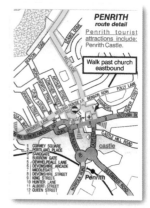

PENRITH route detail

Penrith tourist attractions include: Penrith Castle.

Walk past church eastbound

1 CORNEY SQUARE
2 PORTLAND PLACE
3 SANDGATE
4 BURROW GATE
5 DEWHELPDALE LANE
6 DEVONSHIRE ARCADE
7 MIDDLEGATE
8 DEVONSHIRE STREET
9 KING STREET
10 HUNTER LANE
11 ALBERT STREET
12 QUEEN STREET

castle

Penrith

Accommodation

The Sun Inn, Newton Reigny, Penrith CA11 0AP

Run by: Liz & Keith Dugdale

A 17th century coaching inn, located in this picturesque village. You will find a warm and friendly atmosphere. Superb traditional cask ales, great dining facilities, excellent home cooked food. Relax, enjoy, you've earned it. Deals possible. Two meals for £10 offer.

Rooms: 3 en-suite & 1 family room.
B&B: from £30.
Ev meal & pk lunch: yes.
Secure cycle storage.
On route.
01768 867055
www.thesuninn–newtonreigny.co.uk
info@thesuninn–newtonreigny.co.uk

About the town

A handsome red sandstone market town, Penrith was the capital of the Kingdom of Cumbria in the 9th and 10th centuries, a time when the area was allied to Scotland as a semi-independent part of the Kingdom of Strathclyde. Since it was on the main north-south road it also witnessed more than its fair share of bloody action during border conflicts; the Scots put the town to torch three times during the 14th century alone.

Its early growth was restricted because the town had no water supply, but in 1385 Bishop Strickland diverted Thacka Beck from the river Peterill, an eco-sensitive agreement that allowed the townspeople to draw only as much water daily from the Peterill as would flow through the eye of a millstone (still on view outside the Tourist Information Centre). By the 18th century it was an important cattle market. The oldest streets in the town, Burrowgate and Sandgate, are narrow, unspoilt and 800 years old. Two traditional shops have also survived, as if preserved in aspic: Graham's, Penrith's answer to Fortnum & Mason; and Arnisons, the drapers, established in 1740 in the building that was once the home of Wordsworth's grandparents. The poet and his sister Dorothy attended the Dame Anne Birkett School, now the Tudor Coffee Room, overlooking St Andrew's Churchyard and final resting place of Owen Caesarius, a legendary giant and King of All Cumbria.

They are far from the only famous figures from history associated with the town. As "Guardian of the West March towards Scotland", the Duke of Gloucester plotted his way towards being crowned Richard III from behind the sandstone ramparts of the magnificent Penrith Castle.

It was not all skulduggery though: he also stayed at one of the pubs in town and is even said to have had a private underground passage to it so that he could go back and forth unseen. The link is commemorated in the pub's name, the Gloucester Arms, and some of the original stonework is still there – which is scarcely true of the castle which was a ruin by the mid 16th century, donating much of its stonework to the town's buildings.

The Two Lions pub is equally historic while the George Hotel provided lodgings for Bonnie Prince Charlie in 1745, during his ill-fated foray south in search of the crown.

Others linked to Penrith include Mary Queen of Scots, Oliver Cromwell and the writer, Anthony Trollope. The first must have spent most of her life on horseback to get to all the places she is alleged to have visited, though in the case of Penrith the connection is justified. Cromwell occupied the town in 1654 and though the pen is mightier than the sword, Trollope is not thought to have caused as much bloodshed. More recently, the area was immortalised in Bruce Robinson's classic film comedy of 1987, 'Withnail and I', in which the area is again traumatised – this time by a pair of drunken wannabe actors.

Above Penrith is Beacon Hill, past which you will shortly be cycling. Beacons have been lit there through the ages to warn of threat of invasion. Its views are stunning.

Things to see

Penrith Museum and Tourist Information Centre
Housed in the former Robinson's School, an Elizabethan building altered in 1670 and a school until the early 1970s. The museum covers the history, geology and archaeology of the Penrith area. Free entry.
01768 867466

St Andrew's Church
The Giant's Grave in the Churchyard is that of Owen Caesarius, the legendary slayer of monsters from Inglewood Forest. The tower is 12th century, the rest dates from 1720, being rebuilt after a fire. The stained-glass windows added in 1870.

Bluebell Bookshop,
Angel Square
01768 866660.

The town's architecture . Take a walk around. Well worth a stopover.

Penrith Castle
Started in 1399, once home to Richard III but abandoned after his death. Free entry.

Where to eat

Fifteen, 15 Victoria Road, welcome addition to the Penrith food scene. Laid back atmosphere. Food is fresh and simple yet inventive. Healthy options and some fine cake. Cycle enthusiasts. **01768 867453**

Bewicks Coffee Shop & Bistro, Princes Court, accomplished and simple; lovely setting, reasonable prices: **01768 864764**

Taste of Bengal, Stricklandgate, solid and unpretentious dishes from a place without pretentions: **01768 891700**

George Hotel, Devonshire St, does everything from lounge snacks to formal restaurant. Reliable and reasonable: **01768 862696**

Peaberrys Restaurant & Cafe, Angel Sq, smart in-and-out eaterie, reasonable prices: **01768 890170**

Platinum Chinese Restaurant, buffet more than adequate - some rave reports from other diners: **01768 210210**

Blue Elephant Café, Angel Sq, vegetarian organic retreat upstairs from the Bluebell Bookshop. New cafe owner: **01768 866660.**
Scotts Fish Restaurant, Sandgate, 53-seat no-nonsense chippie next to the bus station: **01768 890838.**

Cycle Shops

Arragons, Brunswick Road. **01768 890 344**
www.arragonscycles.com

Harpers Cycles, 1-2 Middlegate **01768 864 475**

Accommodation

Strickland Arms, Great Strickland, Penrith, CA10 3DF
Run by: Anton & Penny Flaherty
A delightful diversion close to Ullswater, this warm and friendly pub has lots of character and is in the heart of a picturesque Eden Valley village 5 miles from Penrith. There is a secluded rear garden and a dry-stone walled terraced front, with an abundant display of flowers. Real fires, cask ales, a decent selection of wines to go with homemade food. The menu varies from individual short-crust pies, made fresh to order such as Steak & Ale, Chicken Leek, Mushroom & Smoked Bacon and our very own 'Stricky' Lamb & Ale. Also do more exotic dishes such as Moroccan meat cakes.
5 miles from route in Eden Valley. Route goes near Ullswater
Rooms: 1T, 1D.
B&B: £30-£45.
Evening meal: £6 - £15.
Pk lunch: depends what you want.
Secure lock up bike washing facility.
01931 712238
www.thestricklandarms.co.uk
stricklandarmspenrith@hotmail.co.uk

Albany House, 5 Portland Place, Penrith, Cumbria CA11 7QN
Run by: Susan Bell
Lovely mid-Victorian town house close to town centre. Hospitality tray, drying facilities, secure bike storage. Hearty breakfast and the warmest of welcomes.
Rooms: 2D, 3F.
B&B: £27.50-£40.
Pk lunch: from £2.50.
On route. Pub nearby.
3 star AA Highly Commended
01768 863072
www.albany-house.org.uk
info@albany-house.org.uk

65

Fellfoot, 10 Fell Lane, Penrith, CA11 8AA

Run by: Alasdair & Jackie Rutherford,
Fellfoot Independent is a well recommended hostel facility in the
centre of town 85 km from the start of the C2C. Fellfoot offers
welcoming and budget facilities for those determined souls in transit.
There are four twin rooms, self catering facilities, private garden
and secure Bike Storage. Also offers self-catering or bed and buffet
breakfast accommodation. Availability all year round. We look farward
to seeing you. Enquiries about renting the whole house for weekends
or the week welcome.
Rooms: 4T.
B&B: £20 (bed alone); £23.50 (B&B).
Nearest pub: 2 minutes.
01768 840327
www.fellfoot.com
ajruther4rd@homecall.co.uk

Tynedale Guest House, 4 Victoria Road, Penrith, Cumbria, CA11 8HR

Run by: Marguerite and Thomas Powley
High level of comfort and attention to detail. Quality en-suite
accommodation in a warm and friendly environment offering a
delicious, locally sourced English breakfast. Secure cycle storage; an
excellent pedal-stop for weary C2Cers. Pubs and restaurants all close
by.
Rooms: 1S, 3T, 5D, 2F (4 are en-suite).
Open all year.
B&B: from £29.
Evening meal: pubs.
and restaurants nearby.
Pk lunch: if requested.
Secure cycle parking .
Distance from route: 300 metres
01768 867491
marguerite@tynedaleguesthouse.wanadoo.co.uk
www.tynedale-guesthouse.co.uk

Acorn Guest House, Scotland Rd, Penrith, CA11 9HL

Run by: Joyce & Anita
Cycle friendly, immaculate family run guest house five minutes walk
from the town centre. Sizeable rooms are airy and clean with colour
TV. Full English breakfast using good local produce.
Rooms: 4D,4T,1F.
B&B: £32.50 - £45.
Evening meal: groups only catered for.
Pk lunch:£4.50.
On route. Pub: 50m.
AA 4 stars. Secure lock-up.
01768 868696
www.acorn-guesthouse.co.uk
acornguesthouse@fsmail.net

Abbey House, 7 Victoria Road, Penrith, Cumbria, CA11 8HR
Run by: Mark and Anne Holliday
Secure cycle storage. Pub: 50m. Route: 250m.
Just 5 minutes walk from the town. Located very close to the route.
Four en-suite bedrooms with TVs and tea/coffee trays which can
accommodate groups of up to 12. English breakfast. Secure lock up
for cycles. A warm welcome and big breakfast awaits.
Rooms: 4 D/T two of which can be triples. Available as singles.
B&B: £30-£40.

Packed lunch from £5.
(Evening meal to be had in
nearby pubs and restaurants).
01768 863414
www.abbeyhousebandb.co.uk
anneabbeyhouse@aol.com

Blue Swallow Guest House, 11 Victoria Road, Penrith, CA11 8HR
Run by: Peter and Cynthia Barry
Clean, comfortable rooms, six of which are en-suite and one has
a private bathroom. Colour TV, Tea/Coffee trays. Excellent English
breakfast using local produce. Secure lock up for cycles. Easy access
to eating and drinking establishments. Well recommended with lots of
repeat business.
Rooms: 4D, 4T, 2S, 3F (6 en-suite, one with private facilities).
B&B: £30-£40.
Open all year.
Evening meal: surrounded by pubs
and restaurants.
Pk lunch: £5.
Distance from route: 300m.
Nearest pub: 50m.
01768 866335
www.blueswallow.co.uk
blueswallow@tiscali.co.uk

Caledonia Guest House, 8 Victoria Road, Penrith, CA11 8HR
Ian & Sue Rhind
Family run Victorian town house with good spacious rooms. Good
hearty breakfast in a warm and friendly atmosphere. New flat screen
tellies, tea and coffee making facilities in all rooms. New bike shed.
Rooms: 2D, 3T, 1F.
B&B: £31-£40.
Pk lunch: £5.00.
Pub: 200m
01768 864 482
www.caledoniaguesthouse.co.uk
ian.rhind1@virgin.net

Brooklands Guest House, 2 Portland Place, Penrith, CA11 7QN

Beautiful and recently refurbished Victorian terraced house ideal for exploring Northern Lakes and Eden Valley. Under cover cycle storage and wash and drying facilities, we also offer, tea, coffee and biscuits after a hard day in the saddle. Rooms have fans, fridges, radio alarms, bottled water. Brooklands features in the prestigious Michelin Guide and gained the AA 4* Highly Commended Award for the past four years, putting it in the top 10% in Britain. Hearty Cumbrian breakfast, made with local produce. Also very close to Arragons cycle shop. Credit Cards accepted.

Rooms: 4D, 4T, 2S (6 en-suite).

Open all year.

B&B: from £35 per person.

No evening meal but pubs
and restaurants nearby.

Pk lunch: £5.

Covered cycle storage. On route.

01768 863395

enquiries@brooklandsguesthouse.com

www.brooklandsguesthouse.com

Eden Gate, 5 Victoria Road, Penrith, CA11 8HR

Run by: Lorraine Roberts

'S.Rhodes & party from Teesside left the following note: "Excellent stop for C2Cers – unable to fault." You too can enjoy our comfortable rooms, delicious breakfast, secure cycle parking. Within two to three minutes walk of shops and restaurants. Groups of up to 10 catered for.'

Rooms: 1D, 1T, 2F.

B&B: £28 - £40.

Pub 100m. Drying and secure lock-up.

01768 866538

edengateguesthouse.co.uk

enquire@edengateguesthouse.co.uk

Roundthorn Country House, Beacon Edge, Penrith, CA11 8JS

Run by: Graham Carruthers

A beautiful Georgian mansion with spectacular views of the Eden Valley & Lakeland Fells. All rooms are en-suite with TV and tea/coffee making facilties. The hotel has a licensed bar and is great value for money for a hotel of this class.

Rooms: 7D, 2T, 2F (en-suite).

B&B: £48 - £67 (licensed).

Pk lunch: £7.50.

Evening meal: £8.50 - £10.50.

Distance from C2C: on route.

Pub: 1.5 miles (hotel has bar).

VisitBritain: 5 star accommodation.

01768 863 952

01768 864 100

www.roundthorn.co.uk

info@roundthorn.co.uk

Langwathby

Directions
Last chance to take it easy before the serious stuff starts

- You leave Penrith along Fell Lane before turning right onto Beacon Edge. There are fabulous views from here followed by a long descent to the B6412. Enjoy it while you can; the really serious bit is about to start.
- Around Langwathby are the villages of Great Salkeld, Edenhall and Little Salkeld. If you are overnighting at Great Salkeld (the food at the Highland Drove is exceptional and is in the Michelin good pub food guide) then take a left along the B6412 for 3km. Great Salkeld is a pretty little village and the pub does B&B.

  If you turn right onto the B6412 you are soon in the village of Edenhall, where the Eden Hall Country House offers splendid accommodation and fine cooking. Both villages are close to Langwathby, with its lovely village green and Shepherd pub.

  At Little Salkeld the Atkinson family run an equine centre with accommodation. Clive and Sam are still doing excellent accommodation at Langstanes in the village and perennially popular with C2C regulars.
- There's a railway station that services the popular Carlisle to Settle line. This area is popular for overnight stops because the surrounding villages are well-placed for attacking Hartside and the other hills that make the next section the hardest. Melmerby, on the A686 about 5km from Langwathby, is also popular. There's a pub there, a famous bakery, and now some spectacular places to stay.
- Langwathby was a Viking settlement; Edenhall once boasted a fine stately home; and Little Salkeld had its watermill. They are all close to the Long Meg and Little Meg stone circles.
- Long Meg comprises a megalith at the head of 60 stones. The whole monument is some 360ft (115m) in diameter.

Accommodation

Bank House Farm, Little Salkeld, Langwathby, Penrith CA10 1NN
Run by: Raymond & Nancy Atkinson
B&B, self-catering, camping in converted barns and farm cottages for individuals, families or larger groups. Secure cycle storage.
A warm friendly family welcome awaits. Static 39-foot caravan accommodation now available so can take large groups.
Rooms: lots of accommodation possibilities for individuals and groups.
B&B: £30.
Pub: 1.5 miles.
01768 881257
07878 536892
bankhouseequ@aol.com

The Highland Drove Inn & Kyloes Restaurant, Great Salkeld, Langwathby, Penrith, CA11 9NA

Run by: Donald Newton

A real country pub with open fires, real ale, quality wines and beer garden. Good range of bar food with separate 'Kyloes' restaurant serving eclectic and award winning cuisine. Winner of Cumbria Dining Pub of the Year plus CAMRA's Real Ale Pub of the Year. Also in the Michelin 'Inns with Restaurants' guide. Top spot with well chosen wine list. Donald has also opened a new pub, the Cross Keys, on the edge of Penrith on the A686, near the rugby ground.

Rooms: 3D, 2T.
B&B: £35-£65.
Evening bar meal: 2-courses £12.
Restaurant: 2-courses £18-£20.
Pk lunch: £7.50.
On the alternative route via Kirkoswald.
01768 898349
www.kyloes.co.uk
highlanddrove@kyloes.co.uk

Eden Hall Country Hotel & Restaurant, Edenhall, Langwathby, CA11 8SX

Run by: Paula & Wayne Williams

Star country house hotel in beautiful surroundings. Sky TV, telephone, tea/coffee in all rooms. Great chef. Secure cycle storage and drying facilities. Telephone for brochure. The new owners have introduced a very affordable and high end table d'hote (£19.50 for three courses).

Rooms: 5S, 9D, 7T (E-S).
B&B: from £45.
DB&B: from £59.50.
Evening meal: £7.95-£19.50
(for 3-course set dinner).
Pk lunch: £4.95.
VisitBritain: 2 star hotel.
01768 881454
www.edenhallhotel.co.uk
info@edenhallhotel.co.uk

Langstanes, Langstanes, Culgaith Road, Langwathby, Penrith, Cumbria, CA10 1NA

Run by: Clive Gravett

A comfortable sandstone house on the route. Colour TV, Tea/Coffee making facilities, drying room. Open all year. Secure cycle parking.

Rooms: 2D, 1T - all en-suite.
B&B: £28 pppn.
Evening meal no, although pub is only 150m and serves great food.
Pk lunch: £4.50.
Inspection AIA commended.
On route.
01768 881004
www.langstanes.co.uk
clive@langstanes.wanadoo.co.uk

The Black Swan, Culgaith, Penrith, CA10 1QW

Run by: Joanne Fenn

The Black Swan is three miles outside Langwathby on the B6412 but has a keen following on account of its lovely setting and excellent food. Ingredients are local and Richard the chef/owner also has a smokehouse and makes his own Cumberland sausages. All meat is sourced within 10 miles. The menu is adventurous and when the weather warrants it (much of the time) a roaring log fire welcomes guests, as does some excellent beer.

Rooms: 7 S/D/T.

B&B: from £37.50.

Evening meal: around £16.50 (three courses).

01768 88223

www.blackswanculgaith.co.uk

info@blackswanculgaith.co.uk

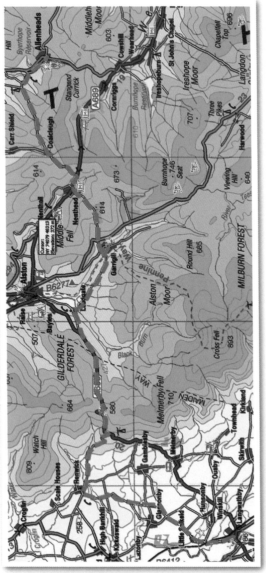

Ordnance Survey © Crown copyright: 100039985

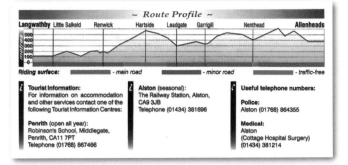

~ Route Profile ~

Langwathby Little Salkeld Renwick Hartside Leadgate Garrigill Nenthead **Allenheads**

Riding surface: ▬▬▬ - main road ▬▬▬ - minor road ▬▬▬ - traffic-free

Tourist Information:
For information on accommodation and other services contact one of the following Tourist Information Centres:

Penrith (open all year):
Robinson's School, Middlegate, Penrith, CA11 7PT
Telephone (01768) 867466

Alston (seasonal):
The Railway Station, Alston, CA9 3JB
Telephone (01434) 381696

Useful telephone numbers:

Police:
Alston (01768) 864355

Medical:
Alston
(Cottage Hospital Surgery)
(01434) 381214

Kirkoswald & Lazonby
Directions
To divert to Eden; or not to divert to Eden. That is the question

- Athough not on the official C2C route, Kirkoswald sees a fair amount of cycle traffic meandering from the set path to enjoy the Eden Valley. When you exit Langwathby you will be presented with choices about what route to take. If you want to go directly to Kirkoswald, bypassing Langwathby, however, you should go left at milemarker 57 and head through Great Salkeld, Lazonby and over the River Eden and into the village.

- All the other options take you into Langwathby, from where you head north towards Little Salkeld and Glassonby. If you are taking this alternative detour to Kirkoswald, leave the main C2C route at milemarker 61.5, head through Glassonby and down the hill into Kirkoswald. Make your way back to the route proper via Viol Moor running parallel to the Raven Beck and onto Four Lane End at milemarker 64.2.

- If you decide to forego the joys of Kirkoswald, just plough straight up the main route and you are soon at Four Lane End.

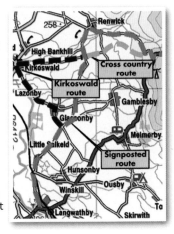

73

- At Four Lane End you can turn right onto the cross-country route over Hartside, but if you do, be warned, you will be pushing or carrying your bike for a lot of the stretch.
- The alternative takes you to Renwick, a winding and steep ascent (I suspect I am not the only cyclist to have hopped out of the saddle for a rest a couple of times).

About the village
Tribute to a warrior, king and saint

The village derives its name from St Oswald who was king of Northumberland from 634 to 642, re-establishing Christianity in the region, founding the monastery at Lindisfarne and to whom the local church is dedicated. The church and bell tower are two separate buildings with the bell tower standing atop a conical hill above the church.

Just outside the village is Kirkoswald Castle, said once to have been "one of the fairest fabrics that eyes looked upon, having a great hall, one hundred yards long, ornamented with pictures of all the kings of England". Though not much remains today it is still worth the short walk to visit it.

Raven Beck, which runs through the village and near much of the path back to the main route, once powered three corn mills, a paper mill, and a mill for carding and spinning wool. It is now the centrepiece of a picturesque stroll above the village.

Accommodation

Mains Farm Campsite , Mains Farm, Kirkoswald, Penrith, CA10 1DH
Robert & Julie Pickthall

Small, quiet park just off the C2C route. Tourers, Tents, and Caravans welcome. Heated toilet & Shower block - unlimited free hot showers/drinking water. Bike washing and maintenance facilities available. Packed lunches and hot breakfast available on request. Ideal first night stop for those starting on the west coast, and great resting place before the Hartside climb to Alston. We have five spacious pitches spread over one acre, with 16 amp electrical hook-up and a brand new shower and toilet block sympathetically converted from a redundant stable.

Outstanding location and views. Riverside walks and woodland picnic area on the farm. Within easy walking distance of Kirkoswald, past winner on many occasions of Cumbria's best kept village award, offering a village shop, post office and pub.

Rate Varies - please give them a call.
Open all year.
Pub 1 mile (free transport provided).
Half a mile from the route.
Secure cycle storage.
01768 898342
pickthalls@themains–kirkoswald.co.uk
www.edenvalleycaravansite.co.uk

The Fetherston Arms, The Square, Kirkoswald, nr Penrith, CA10 1DF
Run by: Jennifer Mossop
Over the years the Fetherston has offered a warm welcome, fine food and real ales to passing cyclists. It is a busy local pub and established guesthouse serving an extensive daily menu of traditional food and a choice of three local real ales. All rooms have been recently refurbished to a high standard with en-suite, tea/coffee making facilities and Freeview TV. There are washing/drying facilities as well.
Rooms: 1 deluxe D, 3D, 1S (all en-suite).
B&B: £30-£35.
Pk lunch: yes.

Evening meal: from £7. Extensive menu.
Open all year. Secure cycle storage.
01768 898284
www.thefetherstonarms.co.uk
info@thefetherstonarms.co.uk

Briardale, Seathill, Lazonby, Penrith, Cumbria CA10 1BD
Run by: Lynda Lowthion
Comfortable family run house offering a twin room and one single, so ideal for a small group (there is an additional put-you-up bed for the twin). The village has a couple of pubs / eating places and is a lovely setting. Mrs Lowthion will do supper if given due notice and you are welcome to wash and dry clothing (and even check your emails).
Rooms: 1T, 1S.
B&B: £28.

Evening meal: please give prior notice.
Pk lunch: £4.
Nearest pub: 100m.
On C2C diversion. Secure lock-up, washing and drying.
01768 897162/07917 153464
llowthion@hotmail.com

Edendale B&B, Edendale, Kirkoswald, nr Penrith, CA10 1EN.
Run by: Mrs Jane Cottam
Comfortable en-suite rooms have stunning views, central heating, television and tea/coffee making facilities. The local shop and two pubs/restaurants are less than 5 minutes walk away. Large lounge/dining room with open fire - Happy Cycling.
Rooms: 1T, 1D, 1S (all en-suite).
B&B: £28.
Pk lunch: from £5.

Evening meal: 2 pubs a couple of mins walk.
01768 870127
www.edendalebedandbreakfast.co.uk
info@edendalebedandbreakfast.co.uk

Prospect Hill House, Kirkoswald, Penrith, CA10 1ER

Run by: Hugh & Yvonne Povey

Prospect Hill House is a welcoming family home, built originally in 1860 as a farm house. Situated above the Eden Valley, it commands fantastic views towards the Pennines and Lakeland Fells. Guests are welcome to wander the extensive mature gardens and view our recently planted arboretum.

Rooms: 1D, 1F refurbished en-suites.
B&B: £32. £10 supplement for single. occupancy.
Pk lunch: £5 (with prior notice).
Evening meal: pubs in village nearby
01768 897138 or 07840 205632
www.prospecthillhouse.com
info@prospecthillhouse.com

The Crown Inn, Kirkoswald, CA10 1DQ

Run by: Carole and Peter Atkinson

A warm, welcoming country pub which although it has no accommodation served food all day, from breakfasts to afternoon tea and dinner. Full range of real ales. Open fire and cosy.

No accommodation. Serving food all day from Easter.

Evening meals: all home made from £6.50 to £10.95 for a 10oz rib-eye. Lunch: wide range of choice from paninis to full meal. Afternoon teas. Range of real ales.
01768 870435 or 07846 769226

Ousby & Melmerby

Accommodation

Bradley Foot, Ousby, nr Penrith, Cumbria, CA10 1QA

Run by: Meryl Durdy

18th century farmhouse on outskirts of quiet fellside village, relaxing and peaceful with excellent views. Ideally situated for touring Lakes, Pennines and Northern Dales. Locked building for bikes. Drying facilities. Full English breakfast with locally produced ingredients. Alternative route three miles from the famous Hartside climb.

Rooms: 2D, 1S (1 en-suite).
B&B: £26.
Secure cycle storage. Pub: 100m
Open February-November
01768 881778
bradleyfoot@hotmail.co.uk

Melmerby Hall & Stag Cottage, Melmerby Hall, Penrith,, CA10 1HB
This Grade II listed nine bedroom stately manor and two bedroom
separate cottage works well for large groups who plan to spend some
time in the local area, or for smaller groups (min stay 3 nights). If
your party can fill the bedrooms at either property, then it works out
about the same price as a B&B. Melmerby Hall and Stag Cottage are
in their own sandstone walled grounds entered through an arched
gateway at the edge of the village. The 20 acres of grounds include
an archery lawn and a Victorian castle folly at the foot of the lawn
(converted to children's play area). There is a picnic area and a stone
built barbecue by the edge of the tributary to the Eden River which
flows through the valley. Melmerby
has an award-winning organic village
bakery and nearby pubs and village
shop. For fuller details see the web link
to Rural Retreats (below).

Rooms 6D, 3T at Melmerby Hall and
1D, 1T at Stag Cottage
Rates £25 - £50
Ample parking. 5 bathrooms at
Melmerby Hall and 2 at Stag.
Fishing available. Croquet.
Paint balling (see housekeeper).
Shooting (contact estate office).
Secure cycle store. Linens, welcome hamper including wine and
breakfast items.
https://www.ruralretreats.co.uk/rr/properties/property.
jsf?ref=CU014
info@ruralretreats.co.uk

. . . .

Addingham View, Gamblesby, Penrith, Cumbria, CA10 1JA
Eileen & Alan Cure
Ideal place to stop before the assault on Hartside. This cluster of
villages (Ousby, Melmerby and Gamblesby) is most attractive.
Addingham is an 1860s home in the Eden Valley and Eileen and Alan
have recently opened it. Keen walkers, they look forward to getting to
know C2Cers. The house is just beyond the church and village green,
about 300m after the road bends round to the right. Eileen and Alan
are happy to run you to the nearest watering holes.
Rooms: 1T, 2D.
B&B: £30-£40. £10 supplement for single occupancy.
Evening meal: information given on variety of local pubs. Free
transport provided to and from same.
Pk lunch: around £4.
Secure cycle storage.
Bike cleaning facilities.
01768 881477
www.addinghamviewbandb.co.uk
addinghamviewbandb@gmail.com

Meadow Bank, Melmerby, Cumbria, CA10 1HF
Run by: Mrs. Margaret Morton
Distance from route: 2 miles from the Hartside climb.
Meadow Bank is the last B&B west of Hartside Pass. After a
comfortable sleep and a Cumbrian Breakfast you will be ready for the
rigours of Hartside Summit (1900ft).
Rooms: 1D, 1F (1 en-suite).
B&B: £25.
Pub: 75m, serves good food.
Melmerby Bakery nearby. Secure storage.
01768 881652

Alston

Directions
Up Hartside, and back down again

- Whichever way you go, it is a hard climb from Little Salkeld but
  at the top awaits Hartside Café, a (motor)bikers' haven. At 580
  metres (1900 feet), it is the highest tea shop in England and on a
  fine day you can see across the Solway Firth to Scotland. The views
  of the Eden Valley are terrific: not for nothing was the drive along
  the A686 voted one of the ten best in the world by the AA.
- Your climb is rewarded by one of the best sections of downhill in the
  North West, as the route plunges 1,000 feet into Alston. Near the
  bottom of Benty Hill there is a road on the right heading towards
  Leadgate and Garrigill. You have a choice – take it, or continue the
  delirious descent along the A686 until you get to the handsome
  town of Alston, perched on the edge of the Pennines.

About the village
Picture perfect legacy of the lead mines

Alston sits at 280m (919 feet) above sea level and is supposedly the
highest market town in England. Picture-postcard-pretty and a firm
favourite with outdoor types, it lies in an Area of Outstanding Natural
Beauty (AONB), a solid bastion of civilisation on the edge of one of
Britain's greatest areas of wilderness.

Once a centre for Cumberland wrestling, cattle fairs and races, Alston
is unspoilt by developers and has cobbled streets, 17th century shops
and pubs that hark back to a former age. Naturally it is a magnet for
film makers; Oliver Twist was shot here for television – there is even
an Oliver Twist trail – and Dickens himself visited in the 1830s to
research Nicholas Nickleby.

The town, formed around the confluence of the South Tyne and Nent
rivers, owes much to lead mining, started by the Romans before the
Quakers set up the London Lead Mining Company in the 18th century.
The Mines Heritage Centre has more information.

The mines and their machinery are silent but the scattered hill farms
recall how mining families grew crops to subsidise their
meagre wages.

The heather-clad moors, fells and valleys are alive with curlews, lapwings, peewits, peregrines and grouse, while deer and red squirrel roam this natural fastness.

There is some fine cycling across Alston Moor before you get to Nenthead. You can either take the B6277 past Garrigill or take the more direct A689.

Places to eat

Alston Wholefoods, Front Street (next to Angel pub), Alston.

Run by: Sarah Sawyer

This is a workers' co-operative which stocks delicious local products (and candles), specialising in organic and Fair Trade. Good beers and wines, gourmet ice creams.

01434 381588

www.cybermoor.org

Alston House is now in the hands of seasoned chef, Michael Allchorne (see p81) **01434 382200**

Blueberry's in the Market Place - good meals, snacks and afternoon tea. See below for details **01434 381928.**

The Cumberland Hotel - see entry **01434 381875.**

The Moody Baker - artisan bakery owned by a workers' co-operative specialising in delicious pies, quiches etc and originators of the high-energy Moody Baker Biker Bar **01434 382003.**

The Cumbrian Pantry, Front St. Good home baking. **01434 381406**

Places of Interest

Tourist Information Centre: Town Hall, Front St. **01434 382244.**

South Tynedale Railway Station: England's highest narrow-gauge track runs along 2.5 miles of former British Rail track. There is a tea room at the old station. Runs every weekend April - October plus some weekends in December, and daily during August. 01434 381696 or, for the talking timetable **01434 382828.**

Hartside Nursery Garden: on route one mile from Alston. Rare and unusual alpine plants. **01434 381372.**

The Hub, Station Unit, opposite rail station, Alston. Local history museum with eclectic mix. Entry by donation, run by volunteers. **01434 382244.**

Accommodation

Victoria Inn, Front St, Alston, CA9 3SE
Run by: Steve & Tian Smith
Packed lunch from £3.50
Friendly, family run B&B right in the centre of Alston. Warm, clean and comfortable accommodation offering everything you need. Accepts all major credit cards. Having briefly closed its doors as a pub, the Victoria is now serving again.
Rooms: 4S, 2D, 2F.
B&B: £23-£30.
Full Indian restaurant.
Also doing takeaway. Sunday roasts
Pk lunch: from £3.50
01434 381194
victoriainncumbria@talk21.com

The Cumberland Inn, Townfoot, Alston, Cumbria CA9 3HX
Run by: Guy & Helen Harmer
Voted CAMRA Pub of the Year for the Solway region. All rooms en-suite, bike storage, drying/cleaning facilities. Only stamping point in Alston. Choice of traditional cask ales and home cooked food. Family run.
Rooms: 2D, 1F, 2triple.
B&B: £32-£38.
Evening meal: £6-£15.
Pk lunch: £4.50.
01434 381875
www.cumberlandinnalston.co.uk
stay@cumberlandinnalston.co.uk

Alston House, Townfoot, Alston, CA9 3RN
Run by: Michael & Carole Allchorne

Good food in an attractive setting boasting some fine real ales. Can take groups of up to 17. There's a drying room and safe cycle storage. Michael & Carole have long experience in the catering business and have refurbished the rooms and bathrooms. Roaring fires in the winter.

Rooms: 1D, 3T, 1F.
B&B: £35-£45.
Evening meal: 6-9pm £8-£18.
On route. Fully licensed.
01434 382200
www.alstonhouse.co.uk
info@alstonhouse.co.uk

YHA Alston, The Firs, Alston, Cumbria CA9 3RW
Run by: Phil Webster

YHA Alston, a 30 bedded Youth Hostel provides 3 star affordable dormitory accommodation in the heart of Alston. All bed linen and towels provided. Hot showers and excellent washing and drying facilities. Superb selection of meals or self-catering option. Open all year round.

Rooms: 2X2, 2X4, 3X6 (bunkrooms)
Bed: from £13.95.
Breakfast: £4.65 trad. English.
Evening meal: £10 for 3 courses.
Pk lunch: £4 or £5.10.
Secure cycle storage. On route.
Pub 5 minute walk.
01434 381509 or 07968 132881
Fax 01434 382401
www.yha.org.uk
alston@yha.org.uk

Lowbyer Manor Country House, Hexham Rd, Alston, CA9 3JX
Run by: Richard & Laura Elston

AA 4 star guest house Secure cycle storage. Drying facilities Grade II listed manor house in the heart of a UNESCO Geopark and Area of Outstanding Natural Beauty. The C2C passes close by as well as several circular routes around the Alston area.

Rooms: 1S, 5D, 2T, 1F.
B&B: £33-£55.
Pk lunch: £5.
Distance from C2C Under 1km.
Same for pub.
01434 381230
www.lowbyer.com
stay@lowbyer.com

Alston Training & Adventure Centre, High Plains Lodge, CA9 3DD.

Run by: Dave Simpson

Ideal for campers or group bookings, though Alston Adventure Centre will accommodate individuals or small groups under the right circumstances. This is the ideal half-way stopping place, overlooking the Alston Valley with stunning views. Warm comfortable dormitories, lashings of food, a superb cooked breakfast, self-catering or camping option available.

Rooms: 10 sleeping 3 or more with total of 45 beds. 2 en-suite shower rooms.

Bed: £12 (bedding extra £4).
Breakfast: £5.50.
Evening meal: £8.50.
Pk lunch: £3.50.
Camping: £4.
Distance from route: 1.5 miles on Nenthead-Garrigill road.
1 mile off-road.
01434 381886
www.alstontraining.co.uk
alstontraining@btconnect.com

Deneholme, The Dene, Allendale, NE47 9PX

Run by: Tony & Lynda Becks

Five acres of grounds.

Exclusive use guaranteed for all groups at this comfortable and stylish Edwardian country manor house on the edge of the village of Allendale. The new owner Tony Becks will be running a shuttle service to Allenheads to pick up groups. Allendale is nine miles north east of Alston and about eight north of Allenheads and many might be tempted to cross Hexhamshire Common to Blanchland and the Derwent Reservoir, but this is not an option for fainthearts! There is another option: the B6295. Three Star accommodation set in five acres of woodlands, Deneholme is comfortably kitted out and is the sort of place you might wish to stop at for more than one night. There is an in-house chef and the house is all yours.

Minimum number: 12.

Rooms: 5T, 3S, 1D, 2F.

B&B: 20 persons or more £35; 15-20 - £40; 12-15 - £45.
DB&B: 20 persons or more £45.50; 15-20 - £50.50 - 12-15 - £55.50.

Distance from route: 7 miles - demands a detour out of Alston into prime AONB. Secure lock up. Pubs nearby. Great for groups.

Prices include VAT.
3 star accommodation
01434 618579
www.deneholme.com
or www.beckstraining.co.uk
tony@beckstraining.co.uk

Garrigill

Just before going to press the George & Dragon announced that it was going to re-open from Easter until August 30th, having closed at Christmas. There will be limited snack food pub a full range of drinks. There is a 'Save the George & Dragon' website and petition. The owners have been trying to sell the pub for the past two years but due to popular demand they have kindly agreed to start serving again, at least for the time being. Its future remains in doubt to please join the movement to save this 400 year old watering hole **(http://www.savethegeorgeanddragon.co.uk/)**. There is also an excellent B&B, a camp site and sleeping space at the village hall. One of the villagers is courageously cooking soups and stews at the village hall for hungry C2Cers and there is even talk of transporting folk to Alston for evening drinks if things don't work out.

Garrigill once had a thriving population of 1,000 thanks to the lead mining. Now it is down to less than 200. It looks like the perfect English village, complete with green and post office. Some of the hardest riding is ahead, so for many it makes a natural overnight stop-off, especially if you have slogged all the way from the fells west of Penrith.

For those who like an extra challenge there is the tough route out of the village, up the very steep and rough track onto the B6277, then left onto a forest track and down into Nenthead the hard way.

Accommodation

Eastview, Garrigill, Alston, CA9 3DU
Run by: Lana Dixie
300 year old miner's cottage on the edge of the village green. Immaculate and very comfortable little establishment. TV, DVDs, games, books and maps. Lock-up and drying.
Rooms: 1D, 1T or 1D.
B&B: £25.
Evening meal: please give prior notice.
Pk lunch: £4.50.
On route.
01434 381561
www.eastview-garrigill.co.uk
info@eastview-garrigill.co.uk

Village Hall, Garrigill
Run by: Kit England
Showers, kitchen, space for sleeping, though the old mattresses donated by the fire service for communal use have now gone, so bring your own mat. There's also a campsite round the back. £10 a night for the hall, £5 for the campsite.
01434 381822
kit.england@gmail.com

Nenthead

About the village

Folk in both Nenthead and Allenheads - the next port of call - claim to live in England's highest village. I would be interested to know definitively which is the higher. Either way, Nenthead is 500m above sea level and has a colder climate than Aberdeen. It does seem incredible that only 300 million years ago it was on the equator.

The village was purpose-built for mining in 1825 by the Quaker Lead Company. In addition to housing they provided a reading room, wash-house, public baths and a school for the 1500 employees in the Methodist stronghold. At weekends they ran smallholdings and this way of life lasted for more than 100 years. A decorative fountain in the middle of the village serves as a memorial to R.W.Bainbridge Esq, superintendent of the mine company.

Falling markets destroyed the community, with cheap imports leading to a collapse in prices, and many families emigrated to the USA and Australia at the end of the 19th century. Zinc mining continued until the 1940s and Nenthead Mines eventually closed its last pit in 1961.

Places of Interest

The Nenthead Mines Heritage Centre is a must. They have brought to life the old workings on this 200 acre site and have helped breathe life into a village that history somehow forgot. You can even do some mineral panning and visit the sites on self-guided trails. **01434 382294**

Killhope Lead Mining Centre is off the A689 5km east of Nenthead. Underground visits possible April - Oct. **01388 537505.**

Cycle Repairs

Mark Fearn
The village blacksmith also repairs bikes, stocks spares and will do a breakdown and recovery service if needed
01434 382194/07776 098915
mark@fearn2620.freeserve.co.uk
www.markfearn.co.uk.

Accommodation

The Miners Arms, Nenthead, CA9 3PF
Run by: Alison Clark
Excellent food and good beer at the pub which lays claim to being the highest in England. Alison has done a class conversion of the former bunkrooms into luxy en-suite accommodation. Her family has run the Miners' since 1988, adding a conservatory dining room. Member of the Green Tourism scheme promoted by the AONB.
Rooms: 1T, 1T or triple. B&B: £35.
Evening meal: £5-£12 (average around £6.50). Pk lunch: £4.
On route with secure cycle lock-up and drying facilities.
01434 3821427
minersarms@cybermoor.co.uk
www.nenthead.com

Mill Cottage Bunkhouse, Nenthead, Alston, Cumbria CA9 3PD
Run by: Tim Haldon
Assay House and Mill Cottage bunkhouses are situated at the Nenthead Mines Heritage Centre. Assay House sleeps up to 12 and has a kitchen diner. Mill Cottage sleeps six in beds styled like ship's cabin bunks, with curtains across for privacy and small internal light and shelf. Assay House was once the laboratory of the Assay Master, who analysed ore samples to determine their lead and silver content. Both bunkhouses are available for group bookings and there is a cafe on site and a pub in the village.
Nenthead Mines Heritage Centre is a Scheduled Ancient Monument and in the 19th century was part of one of the largest lead and silver mining and processing areas in the country.
Neanthead is in the North Pennines Area of Outstanding Natural Beauty and is an ideal hub for those wishing to explore the North Pennines. There are walks and the C2C passes the front door.
Beds: 18.
Price per person: £12.
On route. Pub nearby
Drying facilities and secure lock-up .
01434 382 726 / 382 037
Fax 01434 382 043
www.npht.com
bunkhouse@npht.com

Avesgarth B&B, 13 Hillersdon Terrace, Nenthead, CA9 3PG
Run by: Joan Aves
Family run B&B right on the route with secure cycle store and open all year. Shared bathroom with shower plus extra shower room. Guest lounge with tea and coffee making facilities and TV. Children under 12 sharing - half price.
Rooms: 1S, 1D 1T, 1F.
B&B: £25. U-12s half-price.
Pk lunch: £3.75.
On route. 3 mins from pub.
01434 382 656
avesgarth.mysite.wanadoo-members.co.uk
joan@aves.freeserve.co.uk

Cherry Tree Cottage, Nenthead, Alston, Cumbria, CA9 3PD

Run by: Hellen Sherlock

Farmhouse Bed & Breakfast. Fresh farm eggs from the chickens in the garden. Big breakfast if you wish. Vegetarian alternative. Generous accommodation as Hellen refuses to charge extra for single occupancy.

Rooms: 5D/T/Tpl, 2S.
B&B: £22.50. Same for singles.
Secure cycle parking.
Laundry facilities available.
Miners' Arms 3 minutes.
On route.
01434 381434
www.cherrytree–cottage.org

Crookbank Cottage B&B, Nenthead, Alston, Cumbria CA9 3LN

Run by: Russ & Pam Hildreth

Formerly known as Foulard, it is the birth place in 1876 of Millican Dalton, the eccentric professor of adventure. John Wesley preached here before the Methodist chapels were built, when he visited Alston and Nenthead. There is currently one Family room with TV, Play Station 2 with games and DVD films, tea/coffee making facilities. Modern bathroom downstairs with walk in shower, bath and shaver point. Full English breakfast is served in the wood panelled dining room.

Rooms: 1 Family room, 1 double bed.1 single bed and 1 put up bed.
Open all year.
B&B: £25 per person or as a family: £75.
Pk lunch (book in advance): £ 4.50.
Secure cycle storage.
On route.
About half a mile from Miners Arms.
Evening meal: £5.50 to £15 for three courses (book in advance).
01434 381226s
penninecrag@msn.com

YHA Ninebanks, Orchard House, Mohope, Ninebanks, NE47 8DQ

Run by: Pauline Elliott

YHA in former lead miners cottage now available to non YHA members. Self-catering. Licensed premises. Full catering service for pre-booked groups. Book a bed, a room or the whole hostel. Comfortable year round accommodation. If you can't get through by phone then send an email.

Rooms: 26 beds in 6 rooms (2 en-suite).
Beds: £15.95 and under 18's are £11.95.
Secure cycle parking.
6 miles from Coalcleugh; 7 from Alston. Pub 5 miles.
01434 345288
ninebanks@yha.org.uk
www.ninebanks.org.uk

Allenheads

This is an unremitting stretch with the steepest climb directly out of Nenthead, so if you are staying overnight you may wish to sidestep one of those typically generous Cumbrian breakfasts.

Turn left off the A689 after just over a kilometre of hellish gradient, past the disused lead mineshafts, and soon you will be crossing the highest point on the route – Black Hill. At 609 metres (just a tad under 2000 feet) it is 29 metres (nearly 100 feet) higher than Hartside. Once you have conquered the climb past Killhope Law it's plain sailing to Allenheads.

This is a delightful village nestling among the trees. Its focal point is a marvellous little pub called the Allenheads Inn, one of the most popular stop-off points anywhere along the route.

A century ago this prosperous, peaceful little haven was a toneless grey valley of slag heaps shrouded by smog, a mining community that provided one sixth of the nation's lead. It slipped into decline along with the industry, but has revitalised itself. There is now a village Trust, a visitor centre, mining exhibitions, a shop and a café. It is also home to the British Norwegian Ski Club. There are three tow ropes on the run to the top at 540 metres. Annual family membership is £30. Facilities on the piste include a small bait hut where there is a BYO glühwein facility. Apres ski is in the pub.

An ideal place for celebrities, it is usually free of paparazzi and gossip columnists. A popular haunt with the beau monde of Carlisle and Newcastle, Allenheads is again a coming place.

Places of Interest

Woodland Nature Trail - walks that take you around the village.

Old Blacksmith's Shop - smithy with display.

The Allenheads Trust, Allenheads Heritage Centre, **01434 685043**

Accommodation

Thorn Green Accommodation, Thorn Green, Allenheads, NE47 9JQ

Run by: Julie Macdonald
Bunkhouse, campsite and holiday cottage
right on C2C about a mile before Allenheads. Bunkhouse has seating
area and television plus drying room. Locked bike
shed holds 12 bikes.

The Allenheads Inn just up the road provides
evening meals. The bunkhouse is opposite Thorn Green quarry. There
are six beds in each of the two rooms, room for 4 to 6 in the holiday
cottage (ideal for those spending a little more time in the area). There
is also a campsite with showers.

Rooms: 2 (6 bunks in each+2 showers).
B&B: £20.
Pk lunch: give advance warning.
On route.
Pub nearby.
Drying facilities & secure lock-up.
01434 685234
07977 728328
hammershields@btopenworld.com

The Allenheads Inn, Allenheads, nr Hexham, NE47 9HJ

Run by: Ann & Phil Homer
18th century village inn with renowned reputation. A must for many
cyclists who enjoy atmosphere, hospitality and all-round comfort. Fine
ales and big helpings of tasty food. Camra & Good Pub Guide. Single
occupancy restricted during the busy season.
Free accommodation for one person when accompanied by a
full paying guest if both guests have an evening meal in house.
Offer available between October and April inclusive. Please quote
free accommodation at time of booking. This does not include bank
holidays.
Rooms: 1D,4T,2F.
B&B: £30 sharing, £39 single occ.
Meals: main courses £7.50.
On route.
Pk lunch: £4.50.
01434 685 200
www.theallenheadsinn.co.uk
philann@phomer.fsbusiness.co.uk

New Houses, Allenheads, Northumberland NE47 9HX

Pat & Terry McMullon
Warm, spacious and comfortable cottage
with all amenities. Walking distance to pub.
Rooms: 1S, 2T.
B&B: £23-£30.
Pk lunch: from £4.
On route. Drying facilities. Secure lock-up
01434 685 260
zookon@aol.com

Allenheads Lodge, Allenheads, NE47 9HW

Central heating, secure bike lockup, drying room, separate showers. 4 bed new self-catering cottage to rent next to Allenheads Lodge.

Rooms: 4 (total of 24 beds).
B&B: £20.50.
Bed only: £16.50.
Pk lunch: £4.50.
Evening meal: can be arranged.
On route.
Pub: 700m.
0191 564 0291
sbrewis@springboard-ne.org
www.springboard-ne.org

Places to eat

Hemmel Cafe, Allenheads

Run by: Christine Hutchinson

Somewhere between a cafe and a restaurant serving wine, coffee and tea, new owner Christine Hutchinson's home cooking offers up dishes from chicken and pasta bake to steak pie and all-day breakfast. Vanilla sponges and home baked cakes jostle for space in this charming converted cattle byre with its airy courtyard tucked away behind the car park.
Main courses: £5.50-£8.50
01434 685568
www.thehemmel.com
christinehutchinson@hotmail.co.uk

Ordnance Survey © Crown copyright: 100039985

owlands Gill

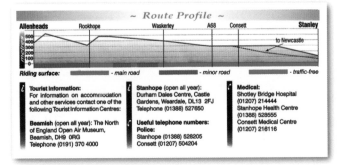

~ Route Profile ~

Allenheads   Rookhope   Waskerley   A68   Consett   Stanley

to Newcastle

Riding surface: - main road   - minor road   - traffic-free

Tourist information:
For information on accommodation and other services contact one of the following Tourist Information Centres:

Beamish (open all year): The North of England Open Air Museum, Beamish, DH9 0RG
Telephone (0191) 370 4000

Stanhope (open all year):
Durham Dales Centre, Castle Gardens, Weardale, DL13 2FJ
Telephone (01388) 527650

Useful telephone numbers:
Police:
Stanhope (01388) 528205
Consett (01207) 504204

Medical:
Shotley Bridge Hospital
(01207) 214444
Stanhope Health Centre
(01388) 528555
Consett Medical Centre
(01207) 216116

Rookhope

The stretch out of Allenheads is almost the last tortuous ascent - and it drags on until you reach the summit at Currick. Then there is a nice stretch of gentle downhill all the way to Rookhope. You soon pass the boundary into County Durham, land of the Prince Bishops - palatinate rulers with absolute authority, equal to a sovereign within the principality. They were granted such power because of the huge strategic importance of the area in the ongoing battle with the Scots.

On your approach you will pass the Lintzgarth Arch, an incongruous and enormous vestige of a bygone era, lying abandoned on the valley floor. The arch carried a 3km horizontal chimney across the valley which replaced the more conventional vertical type when it was realised that a lot of lead literally went up with the smoke. Consequently teams of chimneysweeps were employed to scrape the valuable lead and silver deposits from the chimney once a week. It was a dangerous and filthy job, done by children.

Rookhope is another shrunken mining village. It is also charming, keeping the secret of its hiding place well guarded from sight high above the Weardale Valley. It is hard to imagine that this small group of dwellings was a hive of activity only a few years ago.

In its heyday it supported a surgery, a resident district nurse, vicar, policeman, teashops, several crowded pubs and a busy school. The mining of lead, iron and fluorspar, smelting and the railways totally dominated people's lives.

Today the village is a welcome watering hole and resting place for weary cyclists before the final leg of the C2C journey down to the NE coast. Now there is only a pub (pleasantly refurbished), village shop, post office and working man's club - but a splendid stopping off point, nonetheless.

Accommodation

The Rookhope Inn, Rookhope, Weardale, Co. Durham DL13 2BG

Run by: Tom & Alex Goundry

Cycle friendly and geared to your needs, not least in the shape of the beers available. There's a frequently changed selection of real ale from the likes of Greene King and Black Sheep. The Rookhope Inn is in the Camra Good Beer Guide. A range of traditional dishes is always available, using locally sourced ingredients wherever possible. Delightful setting and great fun place to be.

Rooms: 4T, 1F (all en-suite).
B&B: £32-£35.
Pk lunch: £4.50.
Evening meal and lunches:
Everything from snacks to
full a la carte. Vegetarian options.
01388 517 215
www.rookhope.com
checkin@rookhope.com

The Red Brick Barn, Prydale House, Rookhope, Weardale, DL132DF

Run by: Jane & Andrew Pearce

Offering a high quality, very comfortable converted cattle byre. It is fully self-catering but meals are available to order. Lovely views, farm environment, fuel burning stove and a friendly welcome. Can accommodate 4-16 in the converted barn for £17.50 for a floor for the night and breakfast (bedding provided).

Rooms: 1T, 1D (both en-suite).
Open all year.
Rate: £17.50-£30.
Evening meal: £15 by prior arrangement.
Pk lunch: £5.
Secure cycle parking.
Distance from route: 0.5 miles.
Pub 0.25 miles over fields.
01388 517845 e-mail
jane@prydale.com
www.prydale.com

The Old Vicarage, 1 Stotsfield Burn, Rookhope, Weardale, DL13 2AE

Run by: Colin & Pauline Lomas
Large detached stone-built house in own secluded, tranquil grounds,
orchard garden & courtyard seating to relax in.
Spacious rooms with tea and coffee-making facilities.
Known for 'comfort, excellent food and generous hospitality', according
to the visitors book. Large and comfortable TV lounge, log fire and
board games. You can stroll to the pub and enjoy real ales, in a
convivial atmosphere. There is room in the grounds for tents. It is a
simple & tranquil location and offers a wc, h/c hand basin and shower
with separate sinks for washing-up etc. It is £6.00 pp per night plus
from £2.50 per vehicle/trailer. Please book in advance.

Rooms: 1triple, 2 quad.
B&B: from £32.50.
Pk lunch: £3.50.
Evening meal: £12.50
(including vegetarian option).
On route.
01388 517 375
F:01388 517 701
colin@finetime.wanadoo.co.uk

Eastgate

To get to Eastgate for those heading towards Hole House Bunkhouse
and the comforts of the Cross Keys, take Route 7 signs for Stanhope.
Just outside Rookhope you will see that the C2C branches off to the
left: ignore, and continue straight on, soon crossing the Rookhope
Burn. It's a couple of miles down to the village and then a couple
of miles east to Stanhope, where you rejoin the official route. As
accommodation in this wonderfully remote part of the world is limited,
the addition of Hole House is indeed welcome.

Accommodation

Hole House Bunkhouse B&B, Weardale DL13 2HX
Run by: Nick & Lorraine Thwaites
Charmingly converted bunkhouse on a farm in the village of Eastgate
between Rookhope and Stanhope. Ideal for cyclists and walkers and
very reasonably priced. Secure lock-up for bikes. Pub nearby.
Rooms: 3 quadruples.
Bed: £20 (bunk bed)
Eve Meal: £10 (please pre-book).
Pk Lunch: £4.50 (please pre-book)
Drying facilities & secure lock-up.
01388 517184
holehousebunks@btinternet.com

Stanhope

- From Rookhope you can take the exciting but demanding off-road section which climbs steeply past ruins and heads along the edge of Edmundbyers Common, leading down to the Waskerley Way either by road or across a track – the choice is yours.
- The second choice is to go via Stanhope, one of Weardale's more important and historic little market towns. But if you go this way, remember that you'll be facing a swine of a climb up the B6278 to the Waskerley Way, aptly called Crawley Side.

About the area
Sleepy backwater that reaped the rail reward

Originally a Bronze Age settlement, it was a tiny village around a cobbled market square until the Stanhope & Tyne Railway was built to transport the industrial produce to Consett and Cleveland along the Waskerley Way.

Before the railways, all raw materials were transported by pack horses. Teams of tough little Galloway horses would pick their way over the Pennines and then down into the valleys, the lead horse often having a bell attached to its harness to guide the following horses across the mist-cloaked moors.

> ### Cycle Shop
>
> **The Bike Shop**, Terry & Lorraine Turnbull at Mile Post 100 at the start of the Waskerley Way, 5km from Stanhope. **01388 526434.**

Eating Out

The Bike Stop Stamping post & great teas. Mile post 100

Queen's Head Hotel, Front St. Good pub fare. **01388 528160**

Things to do

Durham Dales Visitor Centre

Castle Gardens. Delightful café. **01388 527 650.**

Fossilised tree at St Thomas's Church 350 million years old, found in 1914 in an Edmundbyers mine.

St Thomas's Church 12th century origins complete with Roman altar and Saxon font.

Accommodation

Belle Vue Farm, Hall Road, Stanhope, Co. Durham DL13 2EZ

Run by: Howard & Linda Lazenby

Howard and Linda created Belle Vue Farm Cottages as a haven for those who love to stay in a peaceful and restful environment with beautiful panoramic views across the Wear Valley and the surrounding wooded and upland areas. Visitors are not just impressed by the external beauty but by the exceptional standard and attention to detail in all rooms to create a warm and welcoming atmosphere. Detached from the farmhouse the cottage style accommodation provides guests with their own privacy. In addition to using the secure cycle store guests may service and wash their bicycles at the workshop. Continental breakfast. No children under 14 years or pets. Private fishing pond.

Rooms: 4D, 1T all en-suite.

B&B: from £62 to £72 per room.

Secure cycle storage. Close to Stanhope branch of route.

Pub: 0.75 miles.

Open all year round.

01388 526225

www.tranquil–life.info

relax@tranquil–life.info

Parkhead Station, Stanhope Moor, Co. Durham DL13 2ES

Run by: Terry & Lorraine Turnbull

Terry & Lorraine worked for Sustrans for many years during the conception of the C2C route. Parkhead Station is specifically designed for cyclists and walkers, renowned within the cycling fraternity and certainly the place to be on the C2C & downhill all the way to the coast! Good home cooked food, licensed, tranquil location, drying room, secure bicycle storage, exceptional service to accommodate individual needs. Take the opportunity to call in and meet us for a well earned break at mile point 100 in our Tea Rooms and experience it for yourself; or book into one of our comfortable rooms, all of which command great views over the North Pennines moorland. Take a virtual tour on the website which also has online booking.

Rooms: 2D, 2F plus The Sleeper (up to six).

B&B: from £30.

Evening meals available (pre-ordering required). Locally sourced produce, please contact us for menu choices and any specific dietary requirements

Pk lunch: £3.50.

Licensed. On route.

VisitBritain 3 stars.

Sustrans C2C t-shirts can be pre-ordered.

01388 526434

www.parkheadstation.co.uk

parkheadstation@aol.com

Queens Head Hotel, 89 Front Street, Stanhope, Weardale, DL13 2UB

John Emerson & Carol Patillo

A small, friendly local pub with bar and dining room, stocking a good pint of real ale. Perennially popular with C2Cers.

Rooms: 4T.
B&B: £25-£30.
Pk lunch: around £5.
Evening meal: 7-8pm £3-£7.
Hotel has public bar.
01388 528 160
www.queensheadstanhope.co.uk
info@queensheadstanhope.co.uk

Edmundbyers & Castleside

Edmundbyers is a popular stopping off point. To get to it, continue along the B6278 instead of turning right for the Waskerley Way. It is buried amongst the heather and wild moorland of Muggleswick Common and is close to the wonderfully picturesque village of Blanchland. Many cyclists continue along the B6278 to Shotley Bridge, bypassing Consett and linking up with the C2C just beyond. If Edmundbyers were to be on the Sustrans map, it would be underneath the superimposed panel showing Consett's town centre.

For those who don't feel like self-catering in the kitchens of the YHA, there is the Punch Bowl pub in the centre of the village, which does good evening meals.

Accommodation

Bee Cottage Guesthouse, Castleside, Consett, Co. Durham, DH8 9HW
Run by: David Blackburn & Irene Mordey
4 star licensed guesthouse. Stunning views. Quiet rural setting.
All en-suite. Clean, comfortable accommodation. Warm welcome guaranteed. Member of Walkers & Cyclists Welcome schemes.
Leave the C2C at Redhouse Farm on the Waskerley Way.
Rooms: 2D, 2T, 4F.
B&B: £35-£45.
Pk lunch: £6.
Evening meal (please give advance warning):
£20 (3 courses + coffee and mints).
On route.
Visit Britain 4 Star & Cyclists Welcome Scheme
4 Star licensed guesthouse.
Stunning views. Quiet rural setting.
01207 508 224
www.beecottage.co.uk
beecottage68@aol.com

Consett

Whether you are coming via Edmundbyers Common or Stanhope, you will shortly be passing the 100 mile point stamping station at the Bike Stop at the start of the Waskerley Way. You can get spares and repairs here, or tea and cake. And it's all down hill from here.

This is a pleasant and easy section of the route, past Muggleswick Common, Waskerley and Smiddy Shaw reservoirs, followed by a quick canter into Park Head Plantation near Bee Cottage, and down to the A68. Beyond here is the magnificent Hownsgill Viaduct, which carried the Stanhope and Tyne Railway Line, Britain's first commercial railway route. There are great views from here across sweeping tracts of deciduous forest and undulating landscape, on the edge of an area that was once the embodiment of heavy British industry.

The pathway is dotted with imaginative Sustrans signage and sculptures cast from industrial relics. Just before Consett are the Terris Novalis sculptures, which overlook the 700-acre site of what was once the mighty Consett Steelworks. The Turner prize winning works - a stainless steel theodolite and an engineer's level by Tony Cragg - are nearly 7m tall, are 20 times life size, and symbolise regeneration in an area convulsed by the death of heavy industry towards the end of the last century. The art works were commissioned by Sustrans and will stand as a monument to this admirable body long after the combustion engine has coughed its last.

"The work sited at Consett marks the watershed between the upland/ moorland landscape and the extremes of the Industrial Age," says the Sustrans website. "Local people see this landmark as a monument to the scale of local industry and its demise - the tragedy that has followed."

Directions

- At Consett the routes part company for the final time; one goes to Sunderland and the other to Newcastle. The split in the route comes just after the Hownsgill Viaduct. On the other side of the lane the route either goes straight on through the centre of Consett to Sunderland. Or you can turn left for Newcastle and Tynemouth. If you go left you will pass the outskirts of Shotley Bridge, whose centre is surprisingly pretty, and then on along the Derwent Walk to Rowlands Gill. I will deal with that later, but for the moment will describe the original route as it progresses gently and scenically into Sunderland. From Consett you head for Stanley, but first you have to get out of Consett, so pay heed to the signs.

- Go round the A692 roundabout, briefly up the left side of Front St before going left between Edith Street and Albert Rd. Cross the latter half way up and go right into Park Rd, cross Front St before heading left and across the B6308, then the path takes you through Leadgate and past the Annfield Plain. Look out for the Kyo Undercurrents sculpture - a series of earth and stone ramps.

Places of Interest

Phileas Fogg - alias Derwent Valley Foods Factory. You will smell it before you see it. Shotley Bridge is an old spa town, well-known for German sword-makers in the 17th century.

C2C Features: dotted along the line are story-boards set on vertical sleepers which interpret the history of the railway. These are chapters taken from a novel, The Celestial Railroad, by John Downie.

Eating Out

Grey Horse, real ales brewed on the premises.
Light lunches and right on C2C route.
Jolly Drovers Pub Leadgate
01207 503 994

Cycle Shops

Consett Cycle Co,
62 Medomsley Rd
01207 581205

Useful Services

The Bike Bus, The Bus Station, Stanley, Co Durham DH9 0TD

Cyclist and bike transport specialists. Transport throughout the UK and size of group no object. Very competitive rates. For more details, see ad on inside back cover.
01207 237424
www.stanleytaxis.co.uk
bike.bus@btconnect.com

Accommodation

Hownsgill Bunkhouse, Hownsgill Farm, Consett, Co Durham DH8 9AA

Run by: John & Stephen Shaw
Kitchen diner seats up to 12. Washing machine/tumble dryer etc.
On the Lydgetts Junction, between the wonderful Hownsgill Viaduct and the Consett section of the Stanhope to Tyne former rail track and Sculpture Trail.
B&B: from £16 (discounts for u-18s).
Rooms: 2 four bed bunks;
1 two bed bunk room; 1D.
Drying area & wet room.
Patio/barbecue area. Car parking.
01207 503597 or 07946 797278
www.c2cstopoff.co.uk
hownsgill_bunkhouse@hotmail.co.uk

Deneview, 15 Front Street, Castleside, Consett, DH8 9AR

Run by: Catherine O'Keefe

Superior B & B accommodation in Castleside village. Colour digital TV. Radio and Tea/Coffee making facilities. Only 25 yards from an excellent pub serving meals each day. 4 Diamond Award.

Rooms: 1D, 1T, 2S (all en-suite).

B&B:£27.50-£35.

Open all year. Secure storage.

Pk lunch £4. Evening meal: local pub.

Pub: 25m.

01207 502925

www.deneview.co.uk

catherine@deneview.co.uk

Crown and Crossed Swords Hotel, Front Street, Shotley Bridge, Consett, Co. Durham, DH8 0HU

Run by: Sheila and Victoria Suddick, with Maureen Cottrell at the pumps

Vibrant pub/hotel in the heart of the scenic village of Shotley Bridge, a short hop from the Consett to Rowlands Gill route and close to the Derwent Valley Rail path. Public Bar, Lounge Bar, Restaurant and ten letting bedrooms. Private car park. Old fashioned, with an emphasis on real ale.

Rooms: 1S, 2D, 4T, 2F (4 en-suite).

B&B: from £25.

Evening meal: yes.

Pk lunch: please order in advance.

Secure cycle storage.

Distance from route: 500m.

01207 502006

Fax: 01207 583111

Consett YMCA, Parliament St, Consett, Co. Durham, DH8 5DH

Run by: Terry Page

There is a drying room, workshop for repairs, colour TV, bar and lounge, pool table, and even a gym if you have the energy left! Ideal for large groups, accommodating up to 45 people. Consett YMCA also organises lots of outdoor activities. Adventure Activities Programmes and holidays a speciality.

Rooms: 10F.

B&B: £15 (or £10 without breakfast).

Evening meal: £5.

Pk lunch: £3.

01207 502680

www.consettymca.org

ymca@derwentside.org.uk

Leadgate

St Ives, 22 St Ives Rd, Leadgate, Consett, Co Durham, DH8 7PY
Run by: Sandra Tilney
Comfortable, modernised old house on the main road bang next to
the route. Ideal stop-off, with en-suite rooms and a big breakfast to
boost you next day. Real welcome for cyclists.
Rooms: 2 triple.
B&B: £25.
Pk lunch: £4.
No evening meal. Pub a few minutes away.
01207 580173

Stanley and Beamish

Stanley is set on a breezy hilltop and commands a bird's eye view of
the whole area. A former mining town situated between Consett and
Chester-le-Street, the name comes from Anglo-Saxon and means
'stony field'. It was first mentioned in 1211 and there are Neolithic
and Roman remains in the area.

Places of Interest

Beamish Museum is England's largest open-air museum and has
a working steam railway, trams, an Edwardian town centre, a
demonstration colliery, a school and a working farm. The C2C route
passes within yards of the entrance gate. **0191 370 4000.**

Tanfield Railway : it is the oldest railway in the world that still
exists. It stops at the Causey Arch north of Stanley - 50m high and
a Scheduled Ancient Monument built in 1728 - and is manned by
volunteers **0191 274 2002.**

Jolly Drovers Maze - built on the site of the former Eden Pit Colliery in
1989. Like the Lambton Worm (see Chester-le-Street) it was designed
by Andy Goldsworthy.

Accommodation

Beamish Mary Inn, No Place, Beamish, Co Durham, DH9 0QH
Run by: Ian Hope
Traditional inn serving six different real ales and now under new
ownership after a couple of years in the doldrums. Ian has plenty of
experience and lots of enthusiasm and there is a big emphasis now on
good, unfussy food. Myra skins the rabbits that go into the pies and
you can get well fed at lunch time. Ian has revamped the place.
Rooms: 1D, 3T, 1Tpl (4 en-suite and one with a private bathroom).
B&B: £25 - £30.
Meals: lunch £10 for 2. Dinner under a tenner.
Distance from route: 500m (behind Beamish Museum)
0191 370 0237 or 07946 730048
ianmhope@hotmail.com

Ordnance Survey © Crown copyright: 100039985

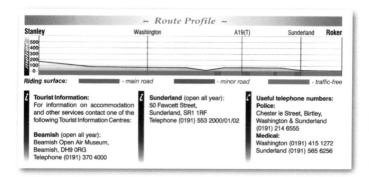

~ Route Profile ~

Stanley · Washington · A19(T) · Sunderland · Roker

500 400 300 200 100 0

Riding surface: ▬▬▬ - main road ▬▬▬ - minor road ▬▬▬ - traffic-free

i **Tourist Information:**
For information on accommodation and other services contact one of the following Tourist Information Centres:

Beamish (open all year):
Beamish Open Air Museum,
Beamish, DH9 0RG
Telephone (0191) 370 4000

i **Sunderland** (open all year):
50 Fawcett Street,
Sunderland, SR1 1RF
Telephone (0191) 553 2000/01/02

i **Useful telephone numbers:**
Police:
Chester le Street, Birtley,
Washington & Sunderland
(0191) 214 6555
Medical:
Washington (0191) 415 1272
Sunderland (0191) 565 6256

Chester–le–Street

Directions

- Just follow the transformed transformers (great steel monoliths sculpted from reclaimed scraps which have assumed iconic status and are now known as the Stanley Sphinxes). Don't forget to look at the metal cows near Beamish. Created by Sally Matthews, they are surprisingly graceful as they stand beside the path, turning grass into rust.

There's also King Coal by artist David Kemp, next to the abandoned railway line at Pelton Fell. This was built of stone from the dismantled Consett railway station bridge and bricks from old kilns, while British Coal provided the crown. It was put together by a stonemason and local volunteers and was, by sheer coincidence, finished on October 15 1992 - the very day of the announcement of the closure of the last pits in Durham's once booming coalfields.

Chester-le-Street is the oldest town in County Durham, and was once a Roman settlement. The Washington Wildfowl and Wetlands Centre is very near the route. This 100-acre waterfowl park designed by Peter Scott has over 1,200 birds and is visited by several mammals, including the scarce water vole.

Places of Interest

The Washington Wetlands Trust 100 acres of magnificent parkland, ponds and hides. 0191 416 5454

Eating Out

The Wheatsheaf Pelaw Grange - **0191 388 3104**
The Barley Mow Browns Buildings - **0191 410 4504**

Cycle Shops

Cestria Cycles 11 Ashfield Terrace - **0191 388 7535**

The Lambton Worm

If you manage to leave the river here in one piece, be thankful! For this is where the Lambton Worm resides (and we are not referring here to the erstwhile politician). The legend runs that a young Lambton lad, fishing in the river against all advice, caught a small worm. In disgust he threw it into a nearby well and went off to fight in the Crusades. On his return the "worm" had grown into a dragon which ravaged the countryside. A witch agreed to slay the beast on condition that Lambton kill the first living thing he met. Unfortunately it was his father, who of course he spared, and so failed to fulfil his side of the bargain, thus nine generations of Lambtons were condemned to meet untimely ends.

C2C Features: the **Penshaw Monument**, a look-alike Doric Temple dedicated to Theseus, was built in memory of John George Lambton, the 1st Earl of Durham.

Sunderland

Directions

The home run

The last leg of the route is scenic as it follows the north bank of the Wear, skirting Washington and passing the Stadium of Light. This route opened in 2000 and is reasonably easy to follow. The end is at the Marina at Roker, a grand spot to finish. Tradition has it that you dip your wheel in the briny - just as you did at the start.

The River Wear

The River Wear in Sunderland is estuarial, much of it protected for wildlife species and habitat including salt marsh. In the summer it is possible to spot salmon, as well as feeding kittiwakes, common terns, cormorants and herons. Much of the riverside is unrecognisable compared to just 20 years ago when it was dominated by collieries, engineering works and dozens of shipyards. The C2C heads eastwards under the Leamside railway line, which crosses the River Wear via the Victoria Viaduct, so named because it was completed on the day of Queen Victoria's coronation in 1838. The elegant design is based upon a Roman viaduct at Alacantra in Spain.

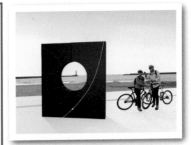

To mark the official end of the C2C 15 years after the route opened, Sunderland City Council officially unveiled a brand new sculpture (above) by local artist Andrew Small. It is the final piece of his triptych of Wearside statues. His work culminates in a giant letter 'O' at Roker marina, and is designed to frame Roker Pier lighthouse for finish line photo portraits of the tens of thousands who come through every year.

About the City

Heritage, history and culture at your seaside rendezvous
Sunderland was once home of shipbuilding, coal-mining, glass blowing and rope making, but it has reinvented itself since becoming a city in 1992, and is now a fascinating mixture of history, heritage and modern facilities to welcome the rider on the last few miles of their voyage. It lies alongside the River Wear, and there has been a major trading hub here since Anglo-Saxon times, when it was one of Europe's major centres of learning and education thanks to the twin monastic settlements of St Peter's (built in 674 with examples of the oldest stained glass in England) and St Paul's. This is where the Venerable Bede wrote the first history of England and it was also here that the art of glass blowing was introduced. By the middle ages, it was one of the biggest and wealthiest towns in England; and that was before the real boom times arrived during the Industrial Revolution, when its population exploded from 15,000 to 150,000 in just a few years. That was when the harbour, created to handle a few small fishing vessels,

blossomed into the biggest international centre for shipbuilding, with as many as 16 working yards. Then, in 1988, more than 550 years of history ended when the last shipyard closed. The coal trains and the heavy industry are long gone, but the grandeur of those Victorian riches can still be seen in echoes of the shipyards visible from the Wearmouth bridge; the elegant architecture, and the country parks at Roker and Mowbray. Now, the dockside that was once filled with soot, coal dust and the sparks flying from the yards, is an elegant sculpture trail where tranquillity and works of art have replaced the thunder of heavy industry. Nowadays, it is a city in tune with nature. The country parks at Herrington and Hetton Lyons are worth the diversion and the route skirts the Wildfowl and Wetland Trust nature reserve at Washington. When you reach the sea you are greeted by

the longest stretch of cityside beach in the UK. Sunderland is also reinventing itself as a modern waterfront city, with bars, restaurants and a thriving nightlife (if you've got the energy for dancing after pedalling over the spine of England) to welcome you. On the way you pass Washington village, the ancestral home of George Washington, winner of the American War of Independence: symbolically completing the loop since Whitehaven, the start of the C2C, is where his grandparents had their home.

Places to Visit

Arts Centre Washington Biddick Lane, Fatfield District 7, Washington, Tyne & Wear, NE38 8AB The Arts Centre Washington is a vibrant focus for arts activities offering a year round programme of arts activities includes exhibitions, theatre, dance, music, festivals, classes and workshops for all ages. **0191 219 3455**
www.artscentrewashington.com | www.artscentrewashington.com

Sights on Your Way

Riverside Sculpture Trail
Between the Wearmouth Bridge and the Marina, the promenade offers a connected trail of specially commissioned artworks in metal and stone that refer back to the city's history and heritage.

Washington Wildfowl & Wetland Centre
Pattinson, Washington NE38 8LE.
This recreated wetland provides a 'stop over' and wintering habitat for migratory waterbirds after their passage over the North Sea and the Wetland Discovery Centre offers both a window on the wide range of wildlife and a programme of art exhibitions. **0191 416 5454**
www.wwt.org.uk

Sunderland Museum & Winter Gardens
Burdon Road, Sunderland SR1 1PP.
Sunderland's museum is hugely popular with visitors of all ages and offers a range of fascinating multimedia installations to tell the city's story from its early foundations to the present day and one of the galleries boasts an extensive collection of paintings by LS Lowry.
0191 553 2323
www.twmuseums.org.uk

Stadium of Light, SR5 1SU.
Magnificent 48,000-seater stadium built on the site of Wearmouth Colliery that closed in 1994. Well worth a visit, tours are available. Alongside is the brand new Olympic standard 50 metre swimming pool, the only one of its kind between Leeds and Edinburgh.
0191 551 5055
www.safc.com

The Sunderland Empire

High Street West, Sunderland SR1 3EX.
Opened in 1907, is the North East's largest theatre and a splendid example of Edwardian architecture. Following a £4.5 million refurbishment the Empire now boasts 21st Century facilities and is the only theatre between Manchester and Edinburgh capable of staging large West End productions.
0870 602 1130
www.getlive.co.uk/sunderland

National Glass Centre

Liberty Way, Sunderland SR6 0GL. Housed in an innovative glass-roofed building on the north bank of the Wear, the National Glass Centre is a fascinating experience and visitors can explore the full history of glass making in the UK and see cutting edge examples of the contemporary glass maker's art. **0191 515 5555**
www.nationalglasscentre.com

Opposite stadium

Park that was the end point of the first steam locomotive railway in the world, the Hetton Colliery Railway, ran 11 miles from Hetton-le-Hole to coal staithes at the River Wear from 1822. The staithes were used until the late 60's.

Wearmouth Bridge

Built in 1796 and seen as a catalyst for the growth of Sunderland. The previous bridge was at Chester-le-Street. There was a pedestrian toll until 1846, and for vehicles until 1885. The adjacent railway bridge opened in 1879 and carries both Metro and conventional rail.

Marine Activities Centre

North Dock, Roker, Sunderland SR6 0PW. The marina at Roker is Sunderland's main focus for all types of water-based sports and leisure activities and boasts an Italian restaurant with panoramic sea views. It's also near your C2C finishing line. **0191 514 1847 86**

City Centre

Across the Wearmouth Bridge stands Sunderland City Centre, incorporating great places to eat, drink and shop and includes bike shops, the Central Railway Station and venues well worth a visit:

St Peter's Church

East of the Wearmouth Bridge, alongside the C2C and the University is St Peter's church, home to the Venerable Bede until he moved to St Paul's in Jarrow. There is now a walkway and cycleway linking the two, and you may spot the small blue signs for it along the rest of the route.

Sunniside & Sunniside Gardens

A large area of public open space in the eastern part of the city centre. The surrounding area is emerging as a cultural quarter with new bars and restaurants and over 100 listed buildings.

Roker Beach and Pier

With its distinctive red and white granite lighthouse, Roker beach provides a wonderful seaside playground and is an ideal place for water sports, with the Marine Activities Centre and other facilities close by.

Places to Eat & Drink

There are a number of public houses near the C2C finishing point. The Harbour View, The New Derby, The Cliff, The Queen Vic, the bar of the Roker Hotel and a few others are all within walking distance. The Smugglers, on the promenade at Roker Beach, was voted the top music venue in Sunderland and they have live music most days of the week. Bar meals are available at most of these pubs. There are also a number of excellent Italians in Little Italy on the promenade and Santini's and Gabrielle's by the Mariott. For snacks, try the Bungalow Café on the cliff top at Roker. It is a well-known landmark, an old-fashioned cafe in a tiny bungalow. Next to it is the famous signpost, marked: "To Beach" (pointing towards the beach), "To Village" (pointing into Roker), "To Bungalow" (pointing to the cafe), and "To Germany" (pointing out to sea).

Seaburn

Shagorika: traditional Indian, reliable feast.

Priti Raj: contempory Indian, highly rated.

Deptford

(over the Queen Alexandra Bridge)

KING'S ARMS, 1 Beech St, Hanover Place, SR4 6BU.
(off Trimdon St behind the B&Q) This is worth the diversion as it's one of the best beer pubs in the North East. It's a ten minute walk from the city centre and is close to the university. Regulars include Timothy Taylor Landlord plus a wide choice of guest beers. There are nine handpumps. Camra pub of the year 2005, 2006 and regional North East winner. Lots of wood panelling, a small snug and lots of pictures of old Sunderland .
0191 567 9804.

SALTGRASS, Hanover Place, SR4 6BY.
Quite why two of Sunderland's best ale houses happen to be tucked behind B&Q just south of the Alexandra Bridge is a mystery that will resolve itself after a pint or two of the many guest beers. Old fashioned and friendly. Beamed ceilings, lots of old pictures. Popular for Sunday lunch.
0191 565 7229.

Roker Pier

Trattoria Due: At the Marina.
Roker Hotel Tavistock: Thai and Italian.
Throwing Stones: Top quality food at the Glass Centre.

THE PROMENADE, Queen's Parade, SR6 8DA
Serves Caledonian, Deuchars and Tetley. Seafront pub with excellent views. Serves good pub grub and upstairs there are four single rooms and three twins.
0191 529 2226.

HARBOUR VIEW, Benedict Rd, SR6 oNL
Good range of beers very well kept. As the pub's name suggests, it has commanding views over the marina and harbour and is a short distance from Roker beach. Specialises in microbreweries from near and far and there's a quiz night Tuesdays and live music on Thursdays.
0191 567 1402.

Accommodation

Lemonfield Hotel, Sea Lane, Seaburn, Sunderland, SR6 8EE

Run by: Gary Hunter

Family run 4 star guesthouse with a good reputation for service and comfort. Parking facilities. Rooms en-suite with colour TV, tea & coffee facilities. Sea views available.

Rooms: 3T, 5D, 2S.
B&B: £25.
On route. Secure storage
Pub: 250m
0191 529 3018
www.lemonfieldhotel.com
gary@lemonfieldhotel.com

Sunderland Marriott, SeaburnQueens Parade, Sunderland, SR6 8DB
Sunderland's only four star hotel is on the seafront overlooking the sandy beaches at Seaburn, two miles north of the city centre and very convenient for the end of the route. A full-service hotel offering modern, high quality accommodation for business and leisure travellers alike. All bedrooms have en-suite facilities and many have sea views. If you want to finish the ride in style, there's a cocktail bar and a good restaurant, private parking and good leisure facilities. The hotel has recently undergone a £0.5 million bedroom refurbishment.
B&B: call to check rates.
0191 529 2041
www.sunderlandmarriott.co.uk
seaburnmarriotthotel@marriott.com

Mayfield Guest House, Sea Lane, Seaburn, Sunderland, SR6 8EE.
Run by: Vincent and Judith Richardson
Attractive building overlooking Seaburn Park and the seafront, close
to some good bars and restaurants on Seaburn, Promenade, only a
few minutes walk. Just 400m away are long stretches of beach which
have been awarded the Blue Flag.
Rooms 4T, 5D, 1F.
B&B £19-£24
City centre: 2 miles 3-stars
0191 529 3345
www.themayfieldhotel.co.uk
enquiries@themayfieldhotel.co.uk

Tavistock Roker Hotel, Roker Terrace, Roker, Sunderland SR6 9ND
Dating back to 1842 this landmark Victorian hotel has recently been
refurbished. Facilities now include two restaurants (an Italian and a
Thai/Chinese), a late bar, conference and banqueting facilities for up
to 350 people, and 57 en-suite rooms, many with views of the North
Sea. The hotel is ideally located for the end of the C2C and is not far
from the city centre.
Rooms: 57.
B&B: from £45, phone for rates.
Evening meal: two restaurants
Packed lunch: by arrangement
0191 567 1786
www.tavistockleisure.com
info@rokerhotel.co.uk

The Balmoral & Terrace Guest Houses, 2/3 Roker Terrace, Sunderland.
SR6 9NB
Run by: Darren Smith
Prominently situated on Roker Sea-Front, within easy access of
Sunderland City Centre, university, Empire Theatre. The Stadium
of Light which is home to Sunderland A.F.C, and The National Glass
Centre and New Marina are only minutes away, as is the finishing
point for the C2C bike ride. For those wishing to dine locally, there are
an array of bars and restaurants close by, including a Chinese and an
Italian doors away. A ten minute walk takes you to the neighbouring
resort of Seaburn, where you will find
Chinese, Italian and Indian food. For
the less adventurous, there are many
seaside fish and chip shops only a
stones throw away.
Rooms 16 rooms
B&B £18-£23
0191 565 9217 or 5650132
www.thebalmoral.supanet.com
thebalmoral@supanet.com

Abingdon Guesthouse, 5 St Georges Terrace, Sunderland SR6 9LX
Run by: Karen Dawson
Very handy for the end of the route. Quiet residential street just off the sea front with plenty of availability at weekends, though can be busy in the week. There is a secure yard in which to store bikes.

Rooms: 6T, 6S
B&B: £22-£33
Pubs and restaurants nearby. On route.
0191 514 0689
www.abingdonguesthouse.co.uk
karen@abingdonguesthouse.co.uk

Cycle Shops

Cycle World, 222 High Street West, Sunderland, SR1 1TZ
0191 5658188 or 5141974,
www.cycleworldshop.co.uk

Peter Darke Cycles, 1/2 John Street, Sunderland, SR1 1DX
0191 5108155, www.darkecycles.com

Halfords Bike Hut, Unit 3, Trimdon Street, Sunderland, SR4 6DW
0191 5140843, www.halfords.com

What next?
Up the coast to join the Reivers route back to the west

There is a wonderful eight mile stretch of coastal cycling between Roker and South Shields, going through Whitburn and Marsden. Known as the Two Rivers Cycleway, this is part of National Route 1, which becomes the Coast and Castles route once across the Tyne, wending a spectacular and beautiful thread up the Northumberland coast and into the Scottish Borders.

It is also the connection between the C2C and Reivers routes, completing the full circle in about 330 miles. This route follows the beautiful beaches on Roker and Seaburn before passing the Souter Lighthouse and Marsden Rock, descending to the old ferry link. Close to the Shields' ferry are a number of great bars overlooking the active Tyne estuary, including the Alum House and bars around Mill Dam / Custom House.

If you finish in Sunderland but your car or train are from Newcastle, the Two Rivers Cycleway is the obvious route. Once at South Shields you have the option of taking the ferry across or taking the pedestrian and cyclists' tunnel (note: do NOT attempt the car tunnel). Also note: the Metro does not allow bicycles, though mainline trains do.

Reivers route starts on page 122

Rowlands Gill to Tynemouth

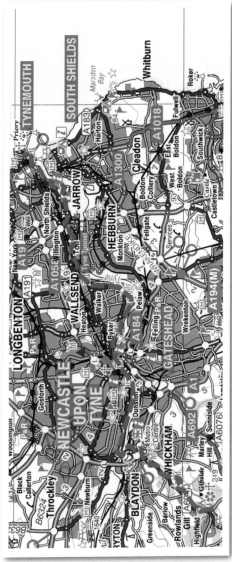

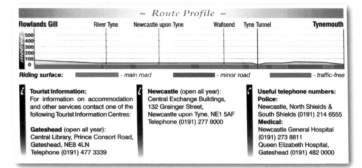

ℹ Tourist Information:
For information on accommodation and other services contact one of the following Tourist Information Centres:

Gateshead (open all year):
Central Library, Prince Consort Road, Gateshead, NE8 4LN
Telephone (0191) 477 3339

ℹ Newcastle (open all year):
Central Exchange Buildings,
132 Grainger Street,
Newcastle upon Tyne, NE1 5AF
Telephone (0191) 277 8000

✆ Useful telephone numbers:
Police:
Newcastle, North Shields & South Shields (0191) 214 6555
Medical:
Newcastle General Hospital (0191) 273 8811
Queen Elizabeth Hospital, Gateshead (0191) 482 0000

Newcastle

Scenic ride to the Toon

The Newcastle route follows the Derwent Walk. This is both scenic and easy to ride, taking you through Hamsterley Mill, Rowland's Gill and through some pretty landscaped areas alongside the river Derwent. When you get to the Tyne go left and over the bridge to the Hadrian's Way path. Although you start off in a rather unpleasant industrial stretch, you are soon back beside the river.

The ride along the Quayside is one of the high points for me. It follows the start of the Coast & Castles route, and the description which follows borrows heavily from my guide book to that magnificent ride from Newcastle to Edinburgh (Coast & Castles - The Complete Guide). I make no apologies.

Newcastle is one of the most happening places in northern Europe (never mind England). A magnet for shoppers and clubbers, diners and drinkers, it boasts some of Britain's finest architecture and has gone through a cultural Renaissance. Recent restoration projects have included Norman fortifications, 16th century merchant houses and the great neo-classical designs of Grainger Town. There are also art galleries, museums and concert venues aplenty.

Newcastle and Gateshead, its neighbour on the south bank of the Tyne, have been voted England's best short break destination. The two towns also teamed up to contend for the European Capital of Culture in 2008, a link symbolised by the arcing strand of the Gateshead Millennium Bridge across the Tyne. Sadly, the gong went to a town arguably in greater need of culture: Liverpool.

Ever since the Romans arrived 2,000 years ago Newcastle has been a hub of trading activity. The town grew up around Pons Aelius, a Roman fortification about 10 miles inland from the North Sea. For the last 800 years a booming trade in wool, leather and coal have brought the city prosperity.

There are now art galleries, museums and concert venues, among them the magnificent Baltic Centre for Contemporary Art on the banks of the Tyne. Of 1930s Art Deco design, the redesignation of this former grain warehouse is typical of the vision and flair that has gone into the area's regeneration.

Places of Interest

Castle Keep, Castle Garth, St Nicholas St. Built by Henry II between 1168-78 on the site of the so-called New Castle, built in 1080 by William the Conqueror's son, Robert Curthose. It was after this edifice that the town was named. The New Castle itself was constructed on the site of the Roman Pons Aelius (Bridge of Hadrian). Admission: £1.50, 50p concessions. **0191 232 7938**

Baltic The Centre for Contemporary Art , Gateshead Quays. Opened in July 2002, BALTIC is the major new centre for contemporary visual art and stands grandly above the water on the south bank. Five galleries and more than 3,000 square metres. It is housed in an old grain store, part of the old Baltic Flour Mills (see above). **0191 478 1810**

The Sage Gateshead, opened 2005. Sir Norman Foster's contribution to the Geordie quayside, a music complex catering for classical, folk, jazz, brass and choral. This is the home of the Northern Sinfonia. Ticket Office - **0191 443 4661**. Switchboard - **0191 443 4666**. Music Education Centre Reception - **0191 443 4627**. Brasserie Bookings - **0191 443 4654**. Coats Desk - **0191 443 4634**. Fax - **0191 443 4551**. www.thesagegateshead.org

Gateshead Millennium Bridge
Takes walkers and cyclists from Newcastle's Quayside across to Gateshead Quays and Baltic Square and the Baltic contemporary art gallery. The bridge opens and closes like a giant eyelid, allowing shipping to pass. Spectacularly lit at night, like many who inhabit these once louche purlieus.

Grainger Town - a rejuvenated architectural treasure trove with some of Britain's greatest examples of Georgian and Victorian architecture, plus many of the city's top shops.

Chinatown - around Stowell St. Restaurant standard is good and prices reasonable. Exotic supermarkets and craft shops.

Pubs

Crown Posada, The Side. Known locally as The Coffin because it is long and narrow, this is probably the city's best pub. There's no TV, and any music comes either from an old gramophone or the mouths of revellers. There are stained-glass windows, interesting ceilings, wood-clad walls and six excellent ales. Legend has it that the pub was bought by a Spanish sea captain for his mistress. **0191 232 1269.**

The Old George Inn, Cloth Market. One of the 'Toon's' oldest establishments, you reach it down a cobbled back alley. Despite being in the middle of the frantic Bigg Market, where every night is like New Year's Eve, it is a grownup drinking spot. **0191 269 3061.**

Duke of Wellington, High Bridge. This pub is a one-room wonder, stocking lots of fast changing ales from all over the country. Used to be run by a 50-stone landlord, one of the biggest men in the world, whose bulk would have barred him from entering the Posada. **0191 261 8852.**

Hotspur, 103 Percy Street. Popular, single-roomed, city centre pub with four guest ales close to the shopping centre. Busy, and busier still when United are on telly. **0191 232 4352.**

Bodega, 125 Westgate Road. According to the Good Beer Guide the highlight of this pub, apart from the range of real ales, is the original twin glass ceiling domes. The pub is a hit with the city's culturati as it stands next to the Tyne Theatre and Opera House. It is a great melting pot as it is also popular with football fans. **0191 221 1552.**

Bridge Hotel, Castle Square. Big pub looking across at the Castle Keep. Nestles into the side of the mighty High Level bridge. Patio garden at the rear, encircled by the old town wall, affords great views of the river. 0191 232 6400.

Where to Eat

Vujon, 29 Queen St. Another classy curry joint. **0191 221 0601.**
Asha Raval, which comes highly rated in Asian circles.. **0191 232 7799.**
Lau's Buffet King, 44-50 Stowell St. **0191 261 8868.**
King Neptune, 34-36 Stowell St. Award winning food. Sumptuous surroundings. You can't go too far wrong anywhere in Stowell St. **0191 261 6657.**
La Riveria, Gateshead Quays. Recent addition to the Gateshead side of the Tyne. Great location and wide choice of Italianate cooking. **0191 477 7070.**
 Marco Polo, 33 Dean St. Friendly, efficient service. Traditional fare, dim lighting. Marco's is an institution. **0191 232 5533.**
Uno's, 18 Sandhill, Quayside. Offers some cheap and cheerful choices. Popular with celebrities. **0191 261 5264.**
Café 21, 19-21 Queen St, Quayside. Simply one of the best restaurants in the north east, you need to book well in advance. **0191 222 0755**
Amer's, 34 Osborne Rd, Jesmond.. Top place serving good and inexpensive grub means you HAVE to book. Cosy and stylish modern cooking in a trendy spot. **0191 281 5377.**
Brasserie Black Door, The Biscuit Factory, 16 Stoddart St. Between Quayside and Jesmond in a 1930s converted factory - the sort of place that is now as voguish as it was hitherto ghastly. Fine cooking in a Modern Art gallery. **0191 260 5411.**
Quay 35, 35 The Side, Quayside. Early evening 2-course special for £11 or £12. Cosy spot, Quay 35 has a good selection of fish, meat and vegetarian options. **0191 232 3848**
Kublai Khan, The Side, Quayside. Only place in the area to do Mongolian food. Served buffet style, you select your ingredients and a Mongol Chinese emperor will cook it for you. **0191 221 1596.**
Heartbreak Soup, Quayside. Latin American/Mexican/ Central American fare. Eclectic and vibey. **0191 222 1701.**

Accommodation

There are plenty of hotels and guest houses. The Jesmond area, just north of the centre, is full of places to stay and lively night spots. If you're overnighting in the city, there are hotels near the waterfront, down on the fashionable Quayside. For a full list of hotels, call the Tourist Information Centre:
0191 277 8000
Newcastle Gateshead Accommodation Guide
ngi@ngi.org.uk
Newcastle Gateshead Initiative
0191 243 8800.
Many cyclists enjoy the Quayside area, close to the Central Station. The atmosphere is vibrant, but the hotels, as in most city centres, can be expensive.

Clifton House Hotel, 46 Clifton Rd, Newcastle upon Tyne, NE4 6XH
Run by: Caterina Love
Elegant country house style hotel in private grounds ideal for end
of C2C or beginning of Hadrians, Coast & Castles or Reivers routes.
Full English breakfast. Private car park, garden and secure lock-up.
Conveniently situated for Newcastle Central Station, Gallowgate
Coach Station and Newcastle Airport. The hotel provides an excellent
base for touring: Hadrian's Wall, Beamish Museum, the market towns
of Hexham and Morpeth as well as the castles of Alnwick, Warkworth
and Bamburgh.

Rooms: 3F, 2T, 2D, 3S.
B&B: from £29 single; £39.50 en-suite.
Evening meal: please give notice.
£16 3-courses with glass of wine & coffee.
Pk lunch: £5
0191 273 0407
cliftonhousehotel@hotmail.com
www.cliftonhousehotel.com

Travelodge, 4 Forster St, Quayside
Family room will sleep three if the double bed is shared.
Rooms:120
B&B: £59.95
0191 261 5432

The Cumberland Arms, James Place St, Ouseburn, Byker, Newcastle upon Tyne, NE6 1LD
Run by: Duty Manager
B&B opened end of May 2009. Stylish yet traditional and vibrant
community pub with broad appeal. The emphasis is on service, good
beer and excellent food. South facing city views from a large outside
drinking area in front of a cobbled cul-de-sac. Interior is original
1920s, with open fires, board games and even a library. There's a
retired miners' dance team and an Irish folk night that's been going
since the 1970s. Featured by Oz Clarke and James May on TV,
described in Lonely Planet magazine by the former as one of the 'best
pubs I've ever been in.'
Rooms: 4D/T.
Competitive prices.
Evening meal: from £5.
Pk lunch: £5.
Secure cycle storage & drying facilities
0191 265 1725
info.cumberland@googlemail.com
www.thecumberlandarms.co.uk

Tynemouth & Whitley Bay

A couple of miles down river on the opposite bank sits Jarrow, home of the Venerable Bede, and the Bede's World Museum. It was also the starting point for the Jarrow March. Two hundred strikers descended upon London in 1936 and made one of the most striking political statements in British working class history.

As you approach the Royal Quays North Sea Ferry Terminus make sure you follow the signs (easily missed) and go to the LEFT of the Wet `n' Wild water centre (you can't miss it - the giant flume tubes look like part of some space-age factory). Follow the path through landscaped public gardens in which an incongruous cluster of wooden sea groynes stand, as if awaiting tidal erosion. Turn left just beyond them, by a faded waysign - do not head back in the direction of the Amsterdam and Bergen ferry terminal - and go through the modern housing estate. To the right, pleasure craft and fishing boats should be bobbing around at their moorings.

Keep following the C2C, Route 72 and Route 10 signs (they are clustered together) and you will find yourself passing through another modern housing estate. You are now in North Shields, erstwhile home of comedian, Stan Laurel.

Following the signs, descend a steep flight of stone steps to the fish quays. You will arrive outside a pub called the Chain Locker, opposite the ferry terminus to South Shields. The view across the Tyne on a good day is worth a pause. You can see, in the far distance, the elegant 19th century façade of the clock tower of South Shields town hall.

Cafes, stores and splendid fish & chip restaurants run the length of the North Shields Quays. This is where Danish and Polish sailors used to integrate vigorously with the local community at a den of iniquity called the Infamous Jungle, now known as the Collingwood Buildings.

You soon round the point where the North Sea meets the Tyne. Welcome to Tynemouth. You pass the 11th century Priory and Castle, and the handsome statue of the man who really won the Battle of Trafalgar in 1805, Admiral Lord Collingwood. Nelson's unassuming and undersung deputy single-handedly took on five French warships for a full hour before the rest of the English fleet caught up. He assumed command upon Nelson's death half-way through the battle, and is Tynemouth's most famous son.

This is a stylish little haven centred upon Front St, a handsome wide avenue built for eating, drinking and promenading. The village is a conservation area of architectural gems from the 18th and 19th centuries. The stretch of shore from here, through Cullercoats and up to Whitley Bay, is known as Newcastle's Côte d'Azur. You will note that there is cycle parking in Tynemouth and Whitley Bay, just over a mile up the coast.

This is where you finish, though there is no obvious place to crack a bottle of Evian Water. No matter. It is a delightful spot and there is bags of accommodation in Whitley Bay, just round the corner (plus a couple of B&Bs in Tynemouth itself).

Don't forget to dip your front wheel in the water.

Places to Eat

Sidneys, Percy Park Rd. Now features in Michelin. **0191 257 8500.**
Giorgio's Pizzeria & Restaurant, Front St. **0191 257 3758.**
Cafe 22, 22a Front St. Good range of healthy options. **0191 257 0090.**
The Gate of India, 40 Front St. **0191 258 3453.**
Gibraltar Rock, Carvery East St. **0191 258 5655.**

Celebrating the End

There are several good pubs in Tynemouth. Here are three recommendations.

Tynemouth Lodge Hotel, Tynemouth Rd. A real locals' pub frequented by the lifeboatmen. Great beers and often very busy. It's at the top of that steep climb out of the North Shields fish quays, on the edge of Tynemouth. Worth tracking back if you have got the energy.

The Turks Head, Front St. Otherwise known as the Stuffed Dog because of Willie the Scottish collie, whose 130 year old taxidermised remains sit in a glass box looking at the bar. Willie came down from the Scottish Borders with a herd of sheep and a shepherd, but somehow got separated from them and spent the rest of his life waiting and pining in Tynemouth for his lost master. A tale of epic proportions told in detail on a plaque. Good Courage Directors, regular guest ales. Food served all day.

Fitzpatricks, Front Street. A handsome establishment, it is one of eight pubs in this small town. Has a changing selection of hand-pulled ales. Food served.

Whitley Bay and Tynemouth adjoin each other so are equally suitable for that final night. It is impossible not to notice that this resort, with its Pleasure Dome, Spanish City and seaside villas, is geared up for tourism and little else. Every other building offers food, drink or accommodation - or all three. Whitley Bay is a striking seaside resort, and in the past was a thriving holiday resort for tourists. It is currently attempting to rediscover its former glory, when smart Geordies would jockey for position on Newcastle Coast's promenade.

Pubs

Fitzgeralds. Half-timbered Victorian pub. Good food and drink and a lively night spot.

Briar Dene. `A former tollhouse with a well-earned reputation for good quality beer and food,' according to the Good Beer Guide (CAMRA Books: £12.99). It overlooks St Mary's lighthouse and the sea. Serves good food.

Rockcliffe Arms Attractive one-roomed pub with stained-glass, & two distinct drinking areas separated by a partition. Proper `locals' pub.

Accommodation

For full details see pages 162-163

Marlborough Hotel, 20–21 East Parade, Promenade, Whitley Bay, NE26 1AP 0191 251 3628/F 0191 252 5033

Avalon Hotel, 26–28 South Parade, Whitley Bay, Tyne & Wear NE26 2RG 0191 251 0080/F: 0191 251 0100

York House Hotel, 106–110 Park Avenue, Whitley Bay, NE26 1DN 0191 252 8313/F:0191 251 3953

Park Hotel, Grand Parade, Tynemouth, Tyne & Wear NE30 4JQ 0191 257 1406

The Northumbria, 51 – 52 Victoria Avenue, Whitley Bay, NE26 2BA 0191 252 5265

Oaktree Lodge, 15 Esplanade, Whitley Bay, Tyne & Wear, NE26 2AH 0191 2528587

The Reivers route

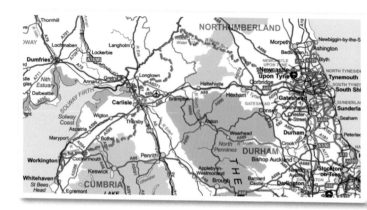

The Reivers Route opened in 1998 and is 173 miles long. It is also known as the 'Return C2C' as it takes you from the end of the west-to-east route all the way back to the start of the C2C. It is a great route in its own right – in some ways superior to the C2C – but it has not had as much attention and money spent on it, is not a fully fledged Sustrans route, and has not been given the mile-by-mile care that has been devoted to the C2C over the years. Some are concerned that not enough is being done to push this beautiful and isolated stretch of northern wilderness. However, the cycle route management unit set up to work closely with local authorities some six years ago along the length of the Reivers, in close co-operation with Sustrans to incorporate the route into the North East Cycle Tourism Strategy, seems to have paid off. The route is once again busier than ever, despite the weather horrors of summer 2008.

As with the C2C the gradients along Reivers work in the cyclist's favour. The route winds its way through some of the wildest and most untouched countryside in the UK. It starts at the mouth of the mighty River Tyne, finishes on the Cumbrian coast and along the way, riders follow the shores of Kielder Water – Europe's largest man-made lake – before crossing the Border for a brief foray into Scotland.

Emerging from the post-industrial and partially regenerated suburbs of Newcastle, the route quickly threads its way into the first gentle then rugged countryside of the Northumberland National Park.

There are fine views across to the towering Cheviots before you become immersed in the forest tracks around Kielder, where there are many options suited to mountain bikers and day tripper alike. After the Borders, Carlisle and down through the Lake District.

This is truly isolated terrain. You could be up in the fastnesses of Sutherland or Ross-shire. But unlike up there, you will stumble across such gems as Hesket Newmarket, with its own excellent micro-brewery, Newcastleton just into Scotland, or Cockermouth and Bassenthwaite. There is a lot of satisfaction to be had from such discoveries.

Maps

Though I provide some basic mapping in this book, and there is some waymarking along the way, you should still get the official route map from Footprint (see right). If you don't mind bulk and cost, the new OS Landranger maps have full route details (though older versions will not have Route 10 marked). OS Landranger maps: (1:50,000) 88, 87, 80, 79, 86, 85, 90 & 89 (in east to west sequence). Maps (£4.95) from:

Footprint:
01786 479866
www.footprintmaps.co.uk

Sustrans:
0117 929 0888

Cordee Books & Maps:
01162 543579
www.cordee.co.uk

Getting there

The Reivers trail starts at Tynemouth Harbour, a scenic spot looking out to the North Sea with the Priory and Castle the first thing you see when you turn your face inland.
To get there, first head for Newcastle. Then you have the choice of riding out to the starting point along the north bank of the Tyne, taking a taxi or taking your car.
Aim for Tynemouth station, and when you get there, turn left into Station Terrace and first right into Huntingdon Place. Straight ahead until you join Front Street, which takes you to the coast. Turn right onto Pier Road and head for the car park. Then let the fun begin.

Travel details are also included at the start of the C2C guide: Pages 9 & 10

Rail

There are direct train services from most cities in Britain to Newcastle Central Station.
Newcastle is served by National Express, Virgin Cross Country and Regional Railways. It takes 2 hours 45 minutes from London, and 1 hour 20 minutes from Edinburgh.
+44 (0)191 221 3156
(station direct line).

To book train seats:

National Rail Enquiry Service
08457 484950

Virgin
08457 222333

National Express
08457 225225

Road

Newcastle is easily accessible by car from all parts of the UK. The A1(M) goes through the middle of it. If you are coming by car, there is limited secure parking in the city centre, near Central Station, for between £5.50 and £7 a day. 0191 243 8294

Waymark

The route is waymarked with a blue direction sign complete with the word REIVERS and the route number, 10. These are posted at junctions and other strategic spots. Occasionally the road surface is signed; sometimes there are just little plastic stickers stuck to gates and lamp-posts. Signage is not always brilliant, but with sharp eyes and the use of a map you should not get lost. Having said that, sections at the beginning and end are notorious for lack of signs; vandals like to trash them, and souvenir hunters snaffle them.

Reivers History

Tales of blood and guts

As you will probably know, the word Reiver means plunderer. The route is named after the murdering bandits who ran a medieval equivalent of Cosa Nostra.

This was the Chicago or Sicily of its time, when marauding clans terrorised both the English and Scottish sides of the Border for 350 years, right up to the 17th century. They lived by cattle rustling, kidnapping, extortion, arson and murder.

The route passes many castles like Bew Castle as well as a number of fortified farmhouses like Askerton Castle, all of which reveal the defensive needs of the area as well as its rich heritage.

Despite the cosy thematising that has been perpetrated by tourism to give the past a false appeal, there is nothing remotely quaint or faintly honourable about Reiving; many of the families were happy to swing both ways, fighting for the English if the price was right, or vice versa.

One family, the Grahams, were so infamous that their surnames were banned by law, so the Grahams changed them to Maharg (Graham backwards), which later also became McHarg.

Indeed, the word 'blackmail' comes from the Reivers: a farmer paid 'blackmail' – rent in the form of cattle instead of the legal 'whitemail', which was paid in silver, to a powerful Reiver who would give him 'protection' in return.

The guilty family names

Archbold; Armstrong; Beattie; Bell; Burns; Carleton; Carlisle;
Carnaby; Carrs; Carruthers; Chamberlain; Charlton; Collingwood;
Crichtons; Crisp; Croziers; Cuthbert; Dacre; Davidson; Dixon;
Dodd; Douglas; Dunne; Elliot; Fenwick; Forster; Graham; Gray;
Hall; Hedley; Henderson; Heron; Hetherington; Hume; Irvine;
Irving; Johnston; Kerr; Laidlaw; Little; Lowther; Maxwell; Milburn;
Musgrove; Nixon; Noble; Ogle; Oliver; Potts; Pringle; Radcliffe;
Reade; Ridley; Robson; Routledge; Rutherford; Salkeld; Scott; Selby;
Shaftoe; Storey; Simpson; Tait; Taylor; Trotter; Turnbull; Wake;
Watson; Wilson; Woodrington; Young.

Tynemouth & Whitley Bay

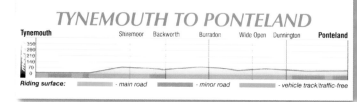

TYNEMOUTH TO PONTELAND

Tynemouth — Shiremoor — Backworth — Burradon — Wide Open — Dunnington — Ponteland

Riding surface: — main road — minor road — vehicle track/traffic-free

About the Town

Those of you doing the round trip will recognise the first three miles of the route, since it is the same as the last three miles of the C2C, but at North Shields it executes a smart right turn and off you go towards the Scottish Border.

There is plenty to do in Tynemouth, which has monuments testifying to a history ranging from Roman times (it is the start of the Hadrian's Cycleway) to the area's recent industrial heritage. Wallsend, nearby, is ideal for the Hadrian's Wall experience. The fort at Segedunum was recently brought back to life at a cost of £9 million, with the only restored Roman bathhouse in Britain.

In medieval times, it was the preferred residence of the queens married to both Edward I and Edward II while their husbands were off bashing the Scots – successfully in the case of the first, less so for his son.

Down river, on the opposite bank, sits Jarrow, home of the Venerable Bede, and the Bede's World Museum. It was also the starting point for the Jarrow March, when 200 protesters descended upon London in 1936 and made one of the most striking political statements in working class history.

For all ACCOMMODATION, PUBS AND EATERY details for
Tynemouth and Whitley Bay: Please see pages 160-163.
THERE ARE LOTS!

Directions

The Footprint map has three large-scale sections showing the best route out of Tynemouth, which I reproduce with their kind permission. There is an alternative route out via Whitley Bay, but the main recommendation is as follows.

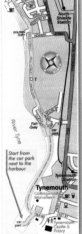

1 Start from the car park off Pier Road, facing the Castle and Priory, and take the path along the estuary. Turn left into Cliffords Fort and immediately right into Union Road, then left through the fish quays of North Shields. There may not be so many fishing boats now, but there are many quality fish and chip shops. Union Quay becomes Bell Street, Liddle Street and finally Clive Street.

2 Go right at the Chain Locker and up the cycle ramp and steps to Tennyson Tce. Follow the signs to Lowson St, going left into an alley and left onto Addison St. At the end of Lowson St go left and then right at the T-junction into Prince Regent Way. At the end of Chirton Dene Way you need to skirt round to the right of the Wet n'Wild tropical indoor water park, with its giant water chutes.

3 Follow the path to the right, along the cycle path parallel with Coble Dene, opposite the huge shopping centre at Royal Quays. This is where the Fjordline and DFDS ferries come in. You now cross Howdon Rd (A187). This brings you to St John's Green. Turn right past Percy Main Station. You will shortly be on the Waggonways, a disused railway line which passes the Stephenson Railway Museum. The famous family hailed from near Wylam, west of Newcastle on the Tyne and the museum has some original locomotives **(0191 200 7145).**

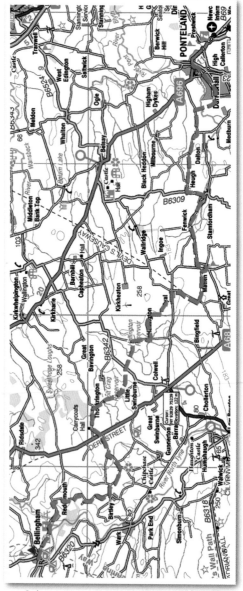

Stamfordham

Directions

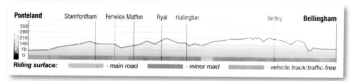

| Ponteland | Stamfordham | Fenwick Matfen | Ryal | Hallington | | | Birtley | Bellingham |

Riding surface: ▬ - main road ▬ - minor road ▬ - vehicle track/traffic-free

Out of the urban sprawl and into the countryside

This is a handsome and planned estate village with a large green (pictured), a pond and a couple of proper English country pubs, the Bay Horse and the Swinburne Arms.

The church may be Victorian but most of the village is stone-built and 18th century.

The name Stamfordham is Old English for `homestead by the stony ford'. It was once part-owned by Balliol College, Oxford.

- Once you are past Shiremoor, you are out of the urban sprawl and can settle down to enjoy the countryside.
- Go left over the level crossing and through Backworth, Burradon and Seaton Burn, taking you past the Big Waters Nature Reserve, Dinnington and up to prosperous Ponteland, where most of the Newcastle United stars live.
- After crossing the golf course you arrive in the village at the Diamond Inn. There is a coffee shop to the left and you can lunch at the pub or the Smithy Bistro, also immediately on your left. But in reality, having covered only 16 miles or so, you are unlikely to require much or want to stop for long. If you do take a break, then there are lots of shops, plus pubs and restaurants to be found here.

Once past Ponteland, you are away from urban life for most of the trip. Go straight across the crossroads but look out for a sign to the right, where you double back on yourself before taking a left hairpin through the smart housing estate of Darras Hall. At the T-junction at the end of the estate go right, then left towards Donkins House Farm before taking a track up to the right.

This will take you via the back lanes to the lovely village of Stamfordham.

Accommodation

Church House, Stamfordham, Northumberland NE18 0PB

Run by: Mrs Viv Fitzpatrick

Pretty village green, old village pubs. 17th century ivory painted stone house of great character on south side of green. Private residence, good breakfast, welcoming hosts.

Rooms: 3T.
B&B: £30-£35.
Pk lunch: £5.
On route.
Pub adjacent.
01661 886 736
07889 312 623
bedandbreakfast@stamfordham.fsbusiness.co.uk

The Bay Horse, Stamfordham, Northumberland, NE18 0PB

Run by: Robin & Julia Carnaffin

Completely and sympathetically refurbished since Robin and Julia took over in 2008. The Bay Horse was once a fortified farm and dates from dates from 1590. All the rooms have been done up. Serves good, locally-sourced food and fine ales and offers 21st century comfort in the heart of the village, overlooking the historic green. There is a new secure lock-up which holds 14 bikes. Offering good lunch deals for cyclists.

Rooms: 5S/T/D, 1F.
B&B: £30-£40 (F £75 and sleeps 5).
Pk lunch: £4.
Evening meal: £5-£15.
VisitBritain 4Stars, 4Diamonds.
01661 886 244
F: 01661 886 940
robin-carnaffin@bay-horse-inn.com
www.bay-horse-inn.com

Wark & Redesmouth

This village is about 2.5 miles from the route. It has a shop, post office, hotel and a pub. The landlord will direct you via a scenic and traffic free lane back onto the route again. Once a Norman frontier town, you enter it over a bridge. Chipchase Castle can be seen from the road. Welcome facilities in an area otherwise bereft of civilisation.

Directions

Road to Delight and beyond ...

Head out of Stamfordham keeping the Bay Horse on your left, passing through the hamlet of Fenwick. You will soon be in Matfen, another immaculate estate village. Here take the right turn signed for Ryal and Capheaton, followed by a right-angled left turn just out of the village. It's a mile or so past the hamlet of Delight until you reach the spendidly named Click 'em In Farm, where you bear right to Ryal.

Just beyond Ryal South Farm there is a track off to the right: if you fancy the off-road option, take it up to Hallington New House, where it joins the road again leading to the cross-roads outside Hallington. Turn right. You can, of course, ignore the off-raod section, and continue to Hallington along the road.

Half a mile outside Hallington there is another off-road option to the left, taking you across a rough farm track and past the reservoir. Be warned – this track can get pretty muddy. This takes you via Little Swinburn and back onto the main route just before Colt Reservoir.

After a quick left-right shimmy to cross the A68, you will soon pass the edge of Birtley. Off to the left is Wark. You will soon come to a junction, with Heugh to the left. Take the right fork, head to Buteland and left onto the minor road, and so steeply down to Redesmouth.

Accommodation

Battlesteads Hotel, Wark, Hexham, Northumberland NE48 3LS

Run by: Richard Slade

A converted 17th-c farmhouse carefully modernised to provide comfortable and eco-friendly surroundings. Very used to having cyclists and will help with repairs. The owners pride themselves on superb authentic English cuisine.

Rooms: 4D, 7T, 2F, Disabled 3T and 1D on ground floor.

B&B: from £40 - £55

PL: £4.75. Evening meals £16.50

Distance from Reivers: 1 mile

(turn left at Birtley)

VisitBritain 4-star inn

01434 230 209

www.battlesteads.com

info@battlesteads.com

The Black Bull, Main St, Wark, Northumberland, NE48 3LG
Run by: Joanne & Darren Tulley
17th century inn on village green now under the ownership of
Richard Slade, who also runs the Battlesteads Hotel round the
corner. Good, locally sourced food and comfortably refurbished
rooms. New cycle lock-up and beer garden.
Rooms: 2D, 2T, 2F.
B&B: £37.50. Single occ. £50. Family room £100.
Evening meal: from £7.50.
Packed lunch: yes.
Distance from route: 1.25 miles.
Drying facilities & secure lock-up.
01434 230239
www.blackbullwark.co.uk
info@blackbullwark.co.uk

Bellingham

About the Village
Where Scots and robbers met their match in stone and blood
This ancient little market town, pronounced "Bellinjum", nestles
at the foot of some of the wildest and most barren fells in
Northumberland. There are medieval references to Bellingham
Castle belonging to the King of Scotland's forester, but sadly no
trace remains.

St Cuthbert's Church is unusual with its stone roof
and extremely narrow windows. Both features were included
as a defence against the marauding Scots who twice burnt it to
the ground. In its graveyard lies the famous "Lang Pack" grave
which is associated with one of Northumberland's most notorious
tales of murder, intrigue and deception. One day a peddler (a
tinker, not a cyclist) came to Lee Hall, the home of a landed local
gentleman and asked if he could leave his backpack there while
he attended to an errand in the village. The maid said yes, and it
was left in the kitchen.

She noted how big and broad the connicle shaped
pack was, but thought no more about it. The gypsy failed to
return that day and during the night she came down with a
candle and noticed the pack had marginally moved. She ran and
fetched old Richards, the wrinkled retainer, who blasted it with a
blunderbuss. There followed much blood and whimpering, then
silence. Inside was the corpse of a criminal whose dastardly plan
was to rob and murder the household in the dead of night. He
got more than he bargained for. His grave lies in the churchyard,
dated 1723. A plot well foiled!

There is also the St Cuthbert's Well, dedicated to the
saint and a welcome addition for thirsty Pennine Way walkers, as
it is right next to the pathway for Britain's most famous walk. On
the edge of the Northumberland National Park on the North Tyne

river, the Bellingham area is well known for its fishing, as it is a major spawning ground for salmon, seat trout and brown trout. It has two caravan sites, a campsite, four pubs and hotels and just about everything else including a haberdashery, gym and library.

The annual agricultural show in the summer (last Saturday in August) is a big attraction with a country fair and Cumberland/ Westmorland wrestling, all done to the skirl of the magnificent Northumbrian pipes.

Directions

The route now goes out of Bellingham following signs for Wark and Hexham. Cross the North Tyne, turn right across Shitlington Common and follow the south bank. You are now in the Northumberland National Park. Continue for about 4 miles to the T-junction where you go right back over the Tyne. There's a climb up to Lanehead then a left. You are on the Falstone road (see p135).

Places of Interest

Hareshaw Linn superb waterfall, a half-mile walk.

St Cuthbert's (Cuddy's) Well Reputed to be healing water.

Tourist Information Centre Main St **01434 220616**

Heritage Centre. Local history. **01434 220050**. Excellent background about Reivers, Border counties railway which ran from Hexham to Bellingham and across the border. Recreation of old mine workings, plus shop of local early 20-c photographer W.P. Collier.

> **Bike Repairs:** Village Country Store, 01434 220027

Accommodation

Riverdale Hall Hotel, Bellingham, Northumberland NE48 2JT
Run by: John Cocker
Country house sporting hotel, own swimming pool, sauna, salmon river, cricket field, golfopposite plus all the cycling and walking routes. Real ale in bar. John Cocker celebrates 30 years at the helm this year.
Rooms: 33.
Ideal for groups.
B&B: from £29-£49.
Pk lunch: from £2.60.
Evening meal: restaurant from £15, bar £9.
2-star Relais Routier Gold Plate for restaurant (only one in Northumberland).
reservations@riverdalehallhotel.co.uk
www.riverdalehallhotel.co.uk
01434 220 254/F: 01434 220 457

133

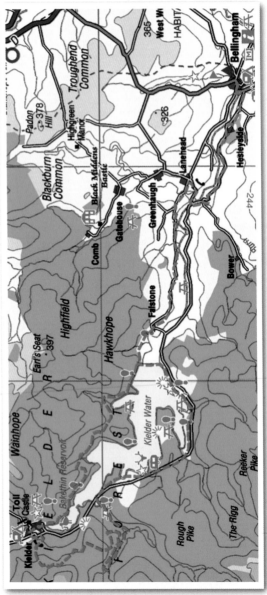

Falstone

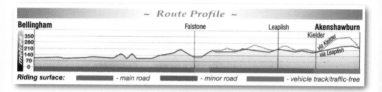

~ Route Profile ~

| Bellingham | | Falstone | | Leaplish | | Akenshawburn |

Riding surface: ▬ - main road ▬ - minor road ▬ - vehicle track/traffic-free

Directions

To find the route out of Bellingham follow the signs for Wark and Hexham. Cross the North Tyne, turn right and follow the south bank. You are now in the Northumberland National Park.

Continue for about 4 miles to the T-junction where you go right back over the Tyne. There follows a climb into Lanehead followed by a left. Close beyond the remains of Tarset Castle you turn onto the Falstone road.

The secluded little hamlet of Falstone lost nearly 80% of its parish under the waters of Kielder Reservoir. Today the village is a tranquil beauty spot surrounded by trees, and is a good stopping place, with post office, shop and pub.

A tributary to the Tyne bubbles its way through the centre of the village and, depending on the time of year, it is possible to see dippers, heron, cormorants, goosanders, and with luck you may witness the miraculous sight of salmon spawning.

About the Village

From the 1st century AD the Northumbrian uplands fell under the control of an expanding Roman Empire. The principal bases of Roman power in the area lay at the forts of Risingham (Habitancum) and High Rochester (Bremenium), both on Dere Street, the main road into Scotland, and to the west at Bewcastle (Fanum Cocidii). Falstone is first recorded in the form 'Foustan' in 1317. This is thought to refer to the 'speckled stone' of the distinctive rocky outcrop, which acquired a religious significance in Medieval times.

Please Read the Following Route Advice Carefully:
It could make or break your trip

The next stage involves serious route choices which could either make or ruin your holiday. Either way, you take a right turn before the bridge in the centre of Falstone (it is marked as a dead-end), carry on down here for 50m and head left down a track to Hawkhope.

- **Your first choice faces you at Hawkhope:**

  1 Go left at the junction and head over the dam to join the road.

  2 Take the forestry track along the north shore of Kielder Water. There are Reivers waymarks and also red arrows marked with the figure 6; both lead the same way. The track is good and is 8km in length, until you get to Gowanburn, where a tarmac road hives off to the left, taking you on a wiggly ride to Kielder village. You pass Kielder Castle and its visitor centre before getting to the village.

- **Here you have another option:**

  3 The sensible one. Take the right turn up past Bell's Burn bridge, Deadwater and Saughtree, then left onto the B6357 and into Newcastleton. This is not the route on the map, but it makes a lot of sense.

  4 Left, then right along Forest Enterprise Route 5c. Be warned, the this path has long, hard climbs.

  If you take Option **1** above, the south shore option at the dam, then do bear in mind that the road can get busy in the summer.

- **There is another choice to be faced:**

  1 Take the off-road Lewis Burn track to Newcastleton, 3km beyond the Leaplish Waterside Park. This is an extremely arduous off-road section through forestry where even experienced hands have been known to get lost.

  2 Carry on along the aforementioned Saughtree road and head out to Newcastleton along the B6357, keeping your wheels firmly on terra firma.

  NB: I would seriously advise anyone with panniers to take the ROAD to Newcastleton, and ignore all suggestions on the Footprint route map trying to lure you into the woods; it is 24km of off-road wilderness, with no services; not even a McDonald's.

  Newcastleton is the only beacon of civilisation (apart from accommodation around Bailey Mill) between Kielder and the village (a seeming metropolis) of Hethersgill, some 30km away.

- **If you are fit and unencumbered, there is yet another tough option:**

  3 Up Serpent Brae. Go left at the Leaplish centre, under the underpass and beetle up the severe incline before turning right and heading through the forest. You should emerge at somewhere called The Forks, where you join the Lewis Burn route to Akenshawburn, where the track crosses the border and snakes along the Scottish side of the Kershope Burn. At Kershope Bridge you can go right to Newcastleton or turn left towards Bailey Mill and yonder hills.

Accommodation

The Pheasant Inn, Stannersburn, Falstone, by Kielder Water, NE48 1DD
Robin Kershaw
Traditional and unspoilt country inn which features in Alistair Sawday's Special Places to Stay. The food is renowned as is the beer: game pies, salmon and local lamb as well as wonderful Northumbrian cheeses. Recently refurbished.
Rooms: 4D, 3T, 1F (sleeps 4).
B&B: £45-£50.
Eve meal: about £17 for 3-courses.
Pk lunch: please pre-order.
Secure lock up. On route.
01434 240382
www.thepheasantinn.com
stay@thepheasantinn.com

Kielder

About the Village

At the head of the reservoir, Kielder was once a wild and uncultivated fastness, surrounded by moors and bogs. It is now a purpose-built forestry village cocooned by alpine spruce and pine trees. Before the turn of the century Kielder Castle, which stands guard over the village, would have been hidden and alone at the valley head. It was built in 1775 by the Duke of Northumberland as his hunting lodge. Shooting parties travelled from London on the sleeper and were met at the station by pony and trap. To carry home a bag of 200 brace of grouse and blackcock in a day was not unusual. The village is a small oasis for the cyclist with a shop, pub and post office. The whole area is now far more accessible as multi-purpose tracks have been put in from the dam almost as far as the village, thanks to the Kielder Partnership. This avoids roads which, during the summer, become horribly busy.

Places of Interest

Kielder Castle Forest Shop, tea room, WCs

Kielder YHA 01434 250195

Kielder Castle Visitor Centre 01434 250 209

Places to Eat

The Anglers Arms **01434 250 072**

Keilder Water

A wild and romantic place, Kielder Water is in the heart of Border Reiver country. It is hard to imagine the cattle rustling, kidnapping and arson that flourished here in the 15th and 16th centuries. Today Kielder's stunning scenery, peace and quiet welcome all visitors. There is a wealth of facilities for the cyclist here. Northumbria Water, who created the reservoir, has been responsible for a good deal of the inspiration behind the Reivers Cycle Route. Sadly, the Reivers Rest at the Leaplish Waterside Park has been closed down for the foreseeable future. Any developments on that front will be posted.

Places of Interest

Tower Knowe Visitor Centre: **0870 2403549**. An Information Centre with extensive gift shop and audio visual exhibition. Situated on the south bank very near the dam wall. Open daily 10-4/5. There is a ferry point, souvenir and fishing shop, exhibition centre, picnic area, extensive lavatory facilities, self-guided trails, a sailing club and a restaurant.

Leaplish Waterside Park: **0870 240 3549**. Heated swimming pool and sauna, campsite, accommodation together with a licensed restaurant, sculpture trail, bird of prey centre, and much more. Open from April-October.

Kielder Ferry Service: 0870 240 3549. 80-seater cruiser takes you round lake, from Tower Knowe to Leaplish to Kielder Castle. Facilities on board include bar, commentary, shop, heated lounge and toilets.

Kielder Water Club: sailing club and yacht club plus a water-ski club. Watercraft hire: **01434 250217**. Range of canoes, kayaks, toppers, wayfarers and dinghies.

Cycling: yes, even cycling. Aside from the Reivers, there are many different routes around Kielder which might interest those of you who are doing a detour here, or perhaps meeting up with the family. Get a 'Cycling at Kielder' brochure from Tower Knowe or Leaplish Waterside Park.

Kielder Castle : **01434 250209**. Former hunting lodge of the Duke of Northumberland overlooks Kielder Village and is open daily from April to October.

Accommodation

Twenty Seven, 27 Castle Drive, NE48 1EQ

Run by: Jill Gregg

Cosy former forester's cottage with multi-fuel stove. Jill lives up the road and serves a splendid breakfast at this relaxing bolt hole in Britain's 'remotest' village. Lock-up and laundry room. Happy to rent place out for self-catering for a minimum of three nights.

Rooms: 1S, 1T, 2F.

B&B: from £30.

Evening meal: pre-order (£8-£10).

Pk lunch: £4.50.

01434 250366 or 250462

www.staykielder.co.uk

jill@staykielder.co.uk

Bike Shops:

The Bike Place. Operates rescue service and repairs, accessories and clothing. Hire service. Big business in a small place. Unit 3, River Mead, Kielder NE48 1HX. **Ian Bell 01434 250 457**

Kielder to Kirklinton

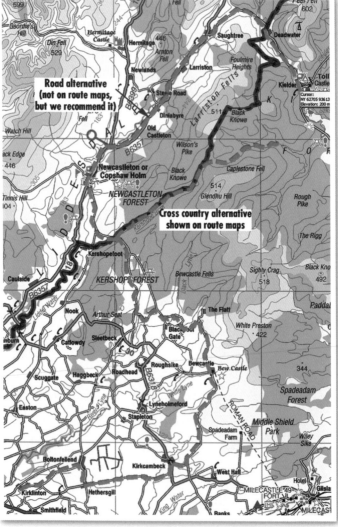

Ordnance Survey © Crown copyright: 100039985

Newcastleton

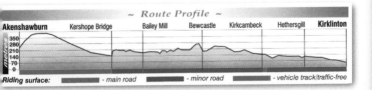

~ Route Profile ~

Akenshawburn · Kershope Bridge · Bailey Mill · Bewcastle · Kirkcambeck · Hethersgill · **Kirklinton**

metres: 350 280 210 140 70 0

Riding surface: - main road - minor road - vehicle track/traffic-free

About the Village

Newcastleton, with its broad Georgian streets and open squares, was purpose designed and built from scratch by the Duke of Buccleuch in 1792. Due to the changes in agriculture there was a need for more village-based employment such as handloom weaving. The houses were built with large windows to let in light for the new cottage industries.

The town has a post office, several pubs, an antique shop, a bank, a grocery and several guest houses. Also the garage will help with bike repairs and there is also the interesting Liddesdale Heritage Centre. If your time and energy allow, don't miss a short detour to Hermitage Castle. This mysterious and magical place not only witnessed long years of turbulent border reiving, but it played host to the tragic Mary Queen of Scots when she snatched two hours' rendezvous with her lover Bothwell.

Accommodation

The Grapes Hotel, 16 Douglas Square, Newcastleton, Roxburghshire, TD9 0QD

Run by: Trevor & Glenys Cambridge
Family run hotel with four bars, excellent bar meals and an 'A La Carte' restaurant. Lock-up for bikes and drying facilities. In a lovely spot; lively or restful - it's up to you.
Rooms: 1S, 2D, 1T, 1D/F, 1X4S, 1 bunkroom.
B&B: from £20.
Pk lunch: made to order.
Meals: from £4.95.
013873 75245/75680
Fax: 013873 75896
www.thegrapeshotel.co.uk
info@thegrapeshotel.co.uk

Liddesdale Hotel, 17 Douglas Sq, Newcastleton, TD9 0QD

Run by: Duty manager
Newly refurbished family hotel now has a
suite, complete with 4-poster. There is a new
emphasis on food and the D, B&B at £45 looks
good value. Fully licensed with a secure lock-
up for bikes. A handsome and solid building
sitting in the main square.
Rooms: 1S, 2D,2T/F, 1 suite.
B&B: from £30 (£45 D,B&B). £40 single occ.
Packed lunch: made to order.
Meals: new fine dining restaurant. £5-£18.
On route.
013873 75255
www.theliddesdalehotel.co.uk
reception@theliddesdalehotel.co.uk

Woodside, North Hermitage St, Newcastleton, Roxburghshire, TD9 0RZ

Run by: Michael Bogg
Red sandstone house built circa 1870 retains many original
Victorian features. All rooms are centrally heated and double
glazed. Large garden and parking for a dozen cars. En-suite
rooms and secure lock-up and washing facilities. 1.5 miles from
7-Stanes mountain bike route (www.7stanes.gov.uk).

Rooms: 1S, 1D, 1T
plus self-catering bungalow for six.
B&B: £25-£27.50.
Pk lunch: £4.
2 pubs near doorstep.
On route.
Cycle storage & wash down facilities.
013873 75431
mandmbogg@sky.com

Sorbietrees, Newcastleton , Roxburghshire, TD9 0TL

Sandy Reynolds
"A warm welcome awaits you at our lovely farmhouse with its
spectacular views, log fires, hearty Aga-cooked breakfasts &
lift to the local pub for evening meal if required."
Rooms: 2D,1T/F.
B&B: £25-£35.
Pk lunch: £4.
Evening meals: no.
On route.
Distance to pub: 2 miles (lift provided)
Drying facilties. Secure lock up.
Bike washing facilities.
VisitScotland Walking/cycling award.
013873 75215
www.sorbietrees.co.uk
sandy.sorbietrees@btinternet.com

Newcastleton high st

Bewcastle
Bailey Mill

At the southern end of Newcastleton take a left, heading up the hill past Sorbietrees and down to Kershope Bridge, right up the steep hill to the telephone box and onward to Bailey Mill. Keep your eyes peeled and follow the Route 10 signs towards Bewcastle. You will soon see a handsome cluster of white buildings that look as if they have been transported from SW France and carefully placed in this harsher clime. This is Bailey Mill, an excellent stop off, whether for food and drink or an overnight stay.

Accommodation

Bailey Mill, Bailey, nr Newcastleton, Roxburghshire, TD9 0TR
Run by: Pam Copeland
Reductions available for large groups, Jacuzzi, sauna, public bar, restaurant and all-round comfort. A great stopping off point in one of the more remote areas of the Borderlands. Secure storage, a hose to wash them down, plus drying rooms. The complex of old farm buildings look as if they could just as easily be in the Dordogne.
Rooms: 2S, 5D, 5T, 4F.
B&B: £28-£38.
Pk lunch: from £4.
Evening meals: from £12-£15
(3 courses).
On route.
016977 48617
www.baileycottages–riding–racing.com
pam@baileymill.fsnet.co.uk

Bewcastle Cross

The famous Bewcastle Cross (left) has survived 1300 years of relentless border weather in St Cuthbert's churchyard.

The church and remains of the castle stand remote and almost alone save for a farmhouse in this forgotten outpost in a great sweep of wild and rugged countryside.

There is a display of interpretative panels nearby in the small Past & Present Heritage Centre. They tell the story of the Anglo-Saxon cross. The runic inscriptions and carving are of a very high quality for this period in history.

Hethersgill

About Hethersgill

There is not a huge amount at Hethersgill, a place whose economy has been traditionally fuelled by peat extraction. You can stop for a pint at the Black Lion pub, which belongs to the same folk who run the Drove Inn at Stapleton, near Hethersgill.

Route: From Hethersgill follow signs to Boltonfellend and head lett to Kirklinton. Here you are on the river Lyne, not far from Longtown. There are lots of tiny communities dotted around here.

Directions

The stretch to Kircambeck is fairly straightforward. After that continue to Hethersgill by heading right at Askerton Castle, then left onto the B6318 and first right at Knorren Lodge.

There is not lot going on here, it's a place whose economy has traditionally been fuelled by peat extraction. You can stop for a pint at the Black Lion pub, which belongs to the same folk who run the Drove Inn at nearby Stapleton.

There are various accommodation choices at places such as Walton and Stapleton – none of them exactly on the route, but all worth a stopover to get a real flavour of the area.

Two possibilities are Low Luckens and New Pallyards. To reach either, take the route past Hethersgill up to Boltonfellend.

Instead of turning left on the signposted route, head straight on, bearing left at the junction with the main road. Continue across the river, taking the second left for New Pallyards, or first right for Low Luckens. If opting for the latter, take a further right after 500m, opposite a farm a kilometre or so up the road; follow a metalled road up to Low Luckens. This delightful backwater is called Roweltown.

> **"Summer is for grazing, but autumn is for raiding"**
> The Reivers were far too busy tending crops and fattening the cattle in summer to be doing any plundering, but as soon as the crops were gathered and the horses fit they would be hot foot across the border to get down to the serious winter business of stealing each other's wives, cattle, sheep & carefully-stored winter goods again.

Accommodation

New Pallyards, Hethersgill, Nr Carlisle, Cumbria CA6 6HZ
Run by: Georgina and John Elwen
Farmhouse accommodation & self catering cottages. Cycles undercover, large groups welcome. National Gold Award.
Rooms: 2S, 2D, 3T, 2F + self-catering units.
B&B: £30-£35.
Pk lunch: £5.
Evening meal: £16 (set menu).
Distance from Reivers: 3km.
01228 577 308
www.4starsc.co.uk
newpallyards@btinternet.com

Low Luckens Organic Resource Centre, Roweltown, nr.Hethersgill, Carlisle, CA6 6LJ
Run by: Jill Jones
Based on an organic farm, they offer self-catering hostel-type accommodation, and lots of organic food. Sleeps up to 12. Can be booked for £100 a night. Four miles NNE of Hethersgill grid ref NY494726 (OS Sheet 86)."
Rooms: 1S, 2F/group.
Self-catering: £12-£15.
£100 for whole place per night or £395 for a whole week.
3 miles from Reivers, nr Roadhead (Stapleton on the Reivers map).
Pub 6km.
016977 48186
lowluckensorc@hotmail.com
www.lowluckensfarm.co.uk

Kirklinton to Longlands

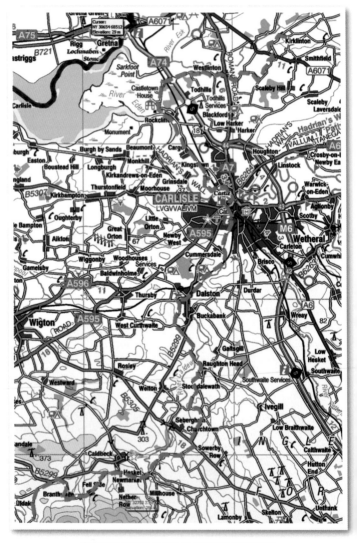

Ordnance Survey © Crown copyright: 100039985

Westlinton/Longtown

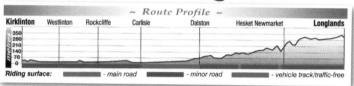

~ Route Profile ~

| Kirklinton | Westlinton | Rockcliffe | Carlisle | Dalston | Hesket Newmarket | Longlands |

Riding surface: ■■■■ - main road ■■■■ - minor road ■■■■ - vehicle track/traffic-free

About the Village
Reiving centre that found respectability

This area which looks so cultivated and prosperous (putting aside for one minute the wretched chapter of foot and mouth disease in 2001) was once so violent that there was no proper settlement outside Carlisle until 300 years ago; that handsome bastion on Longtown's high street, the Graham Hotel, bears the name of the family who settled the town. They were also amongst the most infamous of reiving families (see p.125), whose very surname was at one stage declared illegal. That is the reason there are some 90 pele towers scattered around this area - the only way of staying alive and keeping your few head of cattle was to put them behind lock, gate and thick stone wall when the riders were abroad.

With respectability came not only the Graham Hotel, but high street banks, so if you are running low there are a couple of cash points there. The quickest way to Longtown is to turn right and head up the A6071 fior two miles just beyond Kirklinton, or cross the A7 and turn right just past the Lynebank House Hotel. This takes you onto the Route 7 cycle way, the Lochs & Glens route which connects Carlisle with Glasgow.

Cyclists arriving in Hesket Newmarket

Accommodation

Lynebank Guest House, Westlinton, nr Carlisle, Cumbria CA6 6AA
Run by: Duncan Todhunter
17th century coaching house recently renovated to nine
bedroomed hotel, restaurant and bar. All rooms en-suite.
Licensed. Secure cycle parking in landscaped courtyard.
Kannyble's restaurant has vegetarian options. Free pint for the
first person to guess the provenance of the restaurant name.
Rooms: 3S, 3D, 2T, 1F.
B&B: £22.50 - £40 (with a bridal suite option).
Pk lunch: from £4.50.
Evening meal: £5.85 - £29.50
(the latter is for a 48oz steak).
On route.
VisitBritain 4 stars.
01228 792 820/F: 01228 792 816
www.lynebank.co.uk
info@lynebank.co.uk

Carlisle

Full details in the Hadrians section: Pages 191-196

Directions

The route from Westlinton to the city takes
you down to the edge of the Solway Firth,
where the rivers Eden and Esk meet and
swell a progress across vast acres of mud
and sand until disgorging into the Irish
Sea beyond Bowness and Annan. Here you
pass such erstwhile centres of shipbuilding
as Rockcliffe and other vestiges of a
prosperous past, before cutting through
a large and unattractive industrial estate.
Soon, however, you are in the heart of a
vibrant, welcoming city.

These days this great border
city greets its guests with open arms,
but not so many years ago any visitor
would have been treated with suspicion.
It was the nerve-centre for bitter feuds
and bloody battles created by the long-
running dispute over the border betwen
England and Scotland. Early in its history
it was an important Roman headquarters
for Hadrian's Wall. In 1092 William the
Conqueror's son William Rufus started
to build the castle where later the
unfortunate Mary Queen of Scots was
incarcerated.

During a period of Scots occupation its ruler was one Macbeth; as 'Carluel' it was, according to legend, the domain of King Arthur, and the Emperor Hadrian was perhaps the first to realise that whoever held Carlisle could influence the destinies of both England and Scotland.

Places to stay

Full details in the Hadrians section: Pages 192-195

Angus Hotel & Almonds Bistro, 14 Scotland Rd, Carlisle CA3 9DG
01228 523 546

Crown & Mitre Hotel, English Street, Carlisle, Cumbria CA3 8HZ
01228 525491

Hazeldean Guest House, Orton Grange, Wigton Road, Carlisle, Cumbrian CA5 6JB
01228 711 953

Greysteads Private Hotel, 43 Norfolk Rd, Carlisle CA2 5PQ
01228 522175

Courtfield Guest House, 169 Warwick Road, Carlisle CA1 1LP
01228 522 767

Aaron House, 135 Warwick Road, Carlisle, CA1 1LU.
01228 536 728

Langleigh Guest House, 6 Howard Place, Carlisle, CA1 1HR
01228 530 440

Derwentlea, 14 Howard Place, CA1 1HR
01228 409706/07970 209760

Old Brewery Residences, Bridge Lane, Caldewgate, Carlisle CA2 5SR
01228 597 352

Hesket Newmarket

About the Village

Ask a local the name of an ash tree and he will tell you it is a 'hesh'. Hesket means the place of the ash tree. It is a pleasant village that invites travellers to rest, featuring a medieval stone stall that was used until the late 1900s to tether bulls for the local cattle market. There is a well-stocked village shop, a post office, a couple of guest houses and the Old Crown Inn with its increasingly well-known microbrewery.

You are in the Eastern Fells of the Lake District National Park, an untouched corner of England that proved a magnet for St Mungo in the 6th century, when he came, saw and converted. Many local churches are dedicated to him, usually under his real name: Kentigern (Mungo is a nickname meaning "dear friend"). You are about to tackle the toughest bit of the ride with some challenging up-and-down and majestic views. To the south west you will see the Lake District opening up, with great views of Skiddaw and the Uldale Fells.

Accommodation

Daffodil, Banks Farm, Hesket Newmarket, Cumbria CA7 8HR
Run by: David & Teen Fisher
Dinner: please give advance warning. Otherwise food at Old Crown. Part of a 17th century farm, Daffodil is a luxurious bed and breakfast with fabulous views over the Northern Fells. It offers a private apartment with super king size bed, DVD/TV with iPOD docking, Wifi, bathroom with large walk-in shower and breakfast room. Choice of breakfast and supper service to suit requirements (they have pigs, hens, ducks and sheep on the farm - take your pick!) The owners, who live next door, are happy to run you the half mile or so to the Old Crown if you don't fancy chilling out with a glass of wine in the tranquil garden.
Rooms: 1 double private apartment.
B&B: £110 for the apartment per night.
(10% discount for cyclists or a free packed lunch).
016974 78137
www.daffodilbanksfarm.co.uk
banksfarm@mac.com

Greenhill Farm, Hesket Newmarket, CA 7 8JG.
Run by: Arthur & Joan Todhunter
Splendid little campsite just 250m from the brewery and pub/restaurant. Greenhill is a working farm on the edge of this unspoilt village.
016974 78453

Denton House, Hesket Newmarket, nr Caldbeck, CA7 8JG
Run by: Susan & Alan Armstrong
Friendly atmosphere with home cooking and log fires awaits
everyone in a large 17th century house modernised to 21st
century comforts. Comfortable en-suite rooms with tea /coffee
making facilities. Safe lock up for bikes.
Rooms: 2D, 3T, 3F.
B&B: £27-£32.
Pk lunch: £6.
On route.
Pub nearby (with own brewery).
4 stars. Lock-up & drying facilities.
016974 78415
dentonhnm@aol.com
www.dentonhouseguesthouse.co.uk

Newlands Grange, Hesket-New-Market, nr Wigton, CA7 8HP
Run by: Mrs Dorothy Studholme
Newlands Grange is a working farm looking onto the Caldbeck
Fells. House featuring old oak beams and open fire. Good
home-cooking and a warm welcome awaits all. Transport
to local pub.
Rooms: 1S, 2D, 2T/F .
B&B: £27-£29.50.
Pk lunch: £4.50.
Evening meal: £11.
On route.
Pub 1 mile
016974 78676
studholme_newlands@hotmail.com

Caldbeck

About the Village

Named after the river (Cold-beck), Caldbeck was a thriving
rural industrial centre before steam-power and the Industrial
Revolution. There is still a clog-maker in the village centre.
In 1800 there were no fewer than eight water-powered mills
making bobbins, woollens and grinding corn.
The Priests Mill which has been beautifully restored houses a
craft centre, display area and restaurant with a picture gallery.
In the churchyard is John Peel's grave , the famous Cumbrian
Huntsman, and that of Mary, the Beauty of Buttermere who was
the subject of the novel 'The Maid of Buttermere' by Melvyn
Bragg. Lord Bragg, incidentally, hails from nearby Wigton and is
understandably proud of his local routes (he's a keen cyclist).

Places to Eat

Priests Mill - delicious vegetarian food.
Odd Fellows Arms - pub food & accommodation.

Places of Interest

The Howk: beautiful hidden pathway through the woods to a waterfall and the aforementioned mill. Take a break and have a look...

The Clog Maker, Will Strong: next to the bridge.

Ireby & Longlands

Parkend Restaurant and The Snooty Fox at Uldale are two of notable watering holes in the vicinity, but there aren't that many because this is gloriously open and unspoilt countryside. Just north of Uldale, a tad under two miles from the route, is the charming little vilage of Ireby.

Here the Lion serves excellent pub food and the Woodlands Country House provides hotel accommodation for B&B prices for those wanting to stop off in an old parsonage for a last night before the final stage home. To get to Ireby you simply continue down the B5299 instead of taking the track to Baggra Yeat. To get back onto the route, simply continue through the village (ignore the right turn to High Ireby) and it lies just beyond Ruthwaite).

In my view, it is as good as anywhere on the entire C2C & Reivers route. Pointed peaks emerged from the rolling flow of hills, juxtaposing dark shadows with patches of brilliant sunshine the autumn afternoon I was last on the route.

There are still a couple of serious up-and-downs to come. Take your time - indeed, you will have to, courtesy of the topography - through Fellside, Branthwaite and Langlands.

But once you have got to Bewaldeth it is fairly easy riding into Cockermouth, a delightful stop-off for those who fancy a leisurely finish.

When you have crossed the A591, just beyond Bewaldeth, continue along the lane until you get to the crossroads, where you turn left to cross the River Derwent before heading right at the next crossroads.

Once you have passed Hewthwaite Hall (on the right) it is plain sailing into Cockermouth, where you arrive perilously close to the Jennings brewery. Those who can avoid such temptations might wish to push on to Workington or Whitehaven, the official finishing point. However, I find Cockermouth quite irresistible - fine ales, great fish and chips and one of the best vegetarian restaurants in Britain (the Quince & Medlar). One could quite easily undo all the benefits of several days hard cycling amongst such temptations.

Accommodation

Woodlands Country House Hotel, CA7 1EX

Run by: Judith Wills & Stephen Ort
This beautiful former parsonage has some stunning views and is in the heart of a totally unspoilt section of the Northern Lakes. Part of the VisitBritain Cyclists Welcome scheme, it is fully licensed and does a splendid 4-course dinner with coffee. In the village and a great spot to spend a last night.
Rooms: 7D/T - 3 of which will convert to triples.
B&B: £35-£43.
Evening meal: £22 for hearty
4 course dinner+coffee.
VisitBritain 4 stars. Fully licensed
016973 71791
www.woodlandsatireby.co.uk
stay@woodlandsatireby.co.uk

Whitefield Cottage, Overwater, Nr Ireby, Cumbria CA7 1HH

Run by: Ron & Heike Howes Superbly and stylishly restored house on the edge of the Caldbeck Fells with stunning views across the back of Skiddaw. Set in four acres of landscaped gardens, Ron is a British canoeing coach and outdoor activities instructor, fisherman and organiser. Plenty of bike storage space.

B&B: £32.50-£40 (£35 for single occ).
Rooms: 1D, 2T.
Evening meal: lifts provided within
5 mile radius to pubs or restaurants.
Storage & plenty of parking space
017687 76357
www.whitefieldcottage.co.uk
info@whitehfieldcottage.co.uk

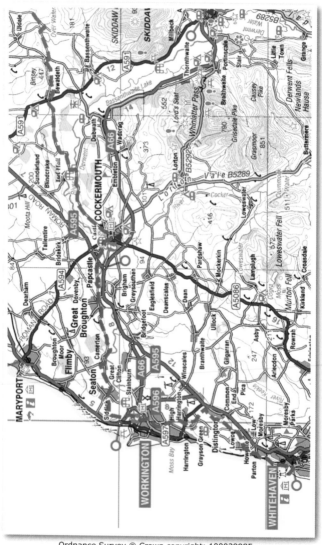

Ordnance Survey © Crown copyright: 100039985

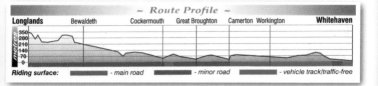

~ *Route Profile* ~

| Longlands | Bewaldeth | Cockermouth | Great Broughton | Camerton Workington | Whitehaven |

350 280 210 140 70 0

Riding surface: — main road — minor road — vehicle track/traffic-free

Directions

- There are some steep bits as you emerge from Longlands, but once you get to Bewaldeth it is fairly easy riding into Cockermouth, a delightful stop-off for those who fancy a leisurely finish.
- Once you have passed Hewthwaite Hall (on your right) it is plain sailing into Cockermouth, where you arrive perilously close to the Jennings brewery.
- Those who can avoid such temptations might wish to push on to Workington or Whitehaven, the official finishing point. However, I find Cockermouth quite irresistible – fine ales, great fish and chips and one of the best vegetarian restaurants in Britain (the Quince & Medlar).
- One could quite easily undo all the benefits of several days hard cycling amongst such temptations.
- This is one of the most attractive towns in the northwest and is just outside the boundary of the Lake District National Park. Perhaps for this reason it is not inundated with tourists. It developed at the confluence of two great salmon rivers – the Cocker, which flows out of lakes Buttermere, Crummock and Loweswater; and the Derwent, which runs through lakes Derwent and Bassenthwaite to Workington.
- It has long fascinated writers, poets and artists and is the birthplace of William and Dorothy Wordsworth – one of the finest buildings here is Wordsworth House, the Lakeland poet's family home, which is now in the care of the National Trust.

Cockermouth

Full details in the C2C section of the guide: Pages 35-38

Directions

The route through Cockermouth differs from the C2C only in that you are heading from north to south, instead of vice versa (the detail map, right, has north at the bottom and south at the top).

You arrive near Jennings Brewery and head up Main Street, passing the Tourist Information and Toy Museum before taking a sharp right and heading towards Popcastle.

There are plenty of things to do and lots of excellent places to eat and drink, which are covered in detail in the C2C section of this guide.

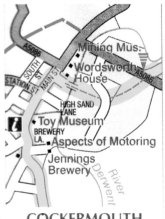

COCKERMOUTH

Places to stay

(Full details in the C2C section of the guide: Pages 37-38)

Riverside, 12 Market St, Cumbria, CA13 9NJ, 01900 827504

Orchard House, Embleton, Cockermouth, Cumbria, CA13 9XP
01900 822189

Allerdale Court Hotel Market Place, CA13 9NQ, 01900 823654

Rose Cottage, Lorton Road, Cockermouth, Cumbria CA13 9DX
01900 822189

Workington

Full details in the C2C section of the guide: Pages 34

Directions

The road from Cockermouth to Workington follows the course of the Derwent via Papcastle, following the C2C in reverse, with the river on your left.

About 4km beyond Great Broughton is Camerton. At the Black Tom climb up to the right and at the old stone bridge hang a left onto the cycle track that takes you to Workington via Seaton. Again, be warned the map, right, shows the route coming in from the north, which is at the bottom.

Places to stay
(Full details in the C2C section of the guide: Page 34)

Morven House Hotel, Siddick Rd, Workington, Cumbria CA14 1LE
01900 602118

Armidale Cottages, 29 High Seaton, CA14 1PD
01900 63704

Whitehaven

Full details in the C2C section of the guide: Pages 15-20

Directions
The final stretch is pretty straightforward. You head out of Workington to Distington where you head for the coast, reaching it at the old Roman fort at Parton Bay and on to Whitehaven. Don't forget to dip your wheel in the briny.

Places to stay
(Full details in the C2C section of the guide: Pages 18-20)

The Mansion, Old Woodhouse, Whitehaven, Cumbria CA28 9LN
01946 61860

Glenfield Guest House, Whitehaven, Cumbria, CA28 7TS
01946 691911

Chestnuts, Low Moresby, Whitehaven, Cumbria, CA28 6RX
01946 61612

Glenard Guest House, Inkerman Terr, Whitehaven, CA28 7TY
01946 692249

Tarn Flatt Barn, Tarn Flatt Hall, Sandwith, Whitehaven CA28 9UX
01946 692162

Chase Hotel, Inkerman Terrace, Whitehaven CA28 8AA
01946 693656

Read Guest House, 5 Cross St, Whitehaven, CA28 7BX
01946 61515

Waverley Hotel, Tangier St, CA28 7UX
01946 694337

The Hadrian's Cycleway

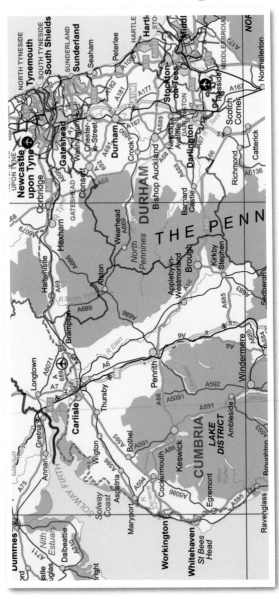

About Hadrian's Cycleway

Hadrian's Cycleway is a 174 mile (280km) National Cycle Network route running through the World Heritage Site and the Solway Area of Outstanding Natural Beauty (AONB). Most of the route is well waymarked and open, and you can get a map and other useful pre-ride items from our website:
www.hadrian-guide.co.uk.
For more background information take a look at the excellent website provided by Hadrian's Wall Heritage Ltd, the company set up to develop the economy of this World Heritage Site. www.hadrians-wall.org. The route was built by Sustrans, the UK's sustainable transport charity.

Cycleway Profiles

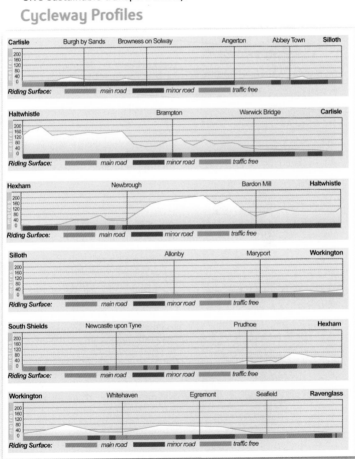

(35 Miles)

Tynemouth & Whitley Bay

Coast and castle

We have pooled these two neighbouring communities so that those wishing to spend a night in the area have a better chance of finding a bed. Tynemouth is limited for accommodation but Whitley Bay abounds with it. The two towns form a significant cycle hub as they are at the beginning and end of several routes in addition to Hadrian's Cycleway: namely the C2C, Reivers and Coast & Castles.

Tynemouth, perched high above the North Sea, was a port in the time of Roman occupation and was used to supply troops manning Hadrian's Wall. Its ruined priory was built by monks from the Holy Island of Lindisfarne in the 7th century. Some 1,200 years later, in Victorian times, the area was filled by a new breed of holidaymaker who arrived on the newly built railway to enjoy the area's sheltered bathing and boating.

This is when Whitley Bay, with its Pleasure Dome, Spanish City and seaside villas, poked its head above the beach front. Whitley Bay is geared up for tourism. Every other building offers food, drink or accommodation - or all three. It is a strikingly traditional English seaside resort and is currently attempting to rediscover its former glory, when smart Geordies would jockey for space on the beach front.

outh Shields to Hexham

Eating places

Sidneys, Percy Park Rd. Now features in Michelin. **0191 257 8500**

Giorgio's Pizzeria & Restaurant, Front St. 0191 257 3758

Cafe 22, 22a Front St. Smart place, trendy & good food. **0191 257 0090**

The Gate of India, 40 Front St. 0191 258 3453

Gibraltar Rock, Carvery East St. **0191 258 5655**

Tynemouth Lodge Hotel, Tynemouth Rd, a real locals' pub frequented by the lifeboatmen. Great beers and often very busy. It's at the top of that steep climb out of the North Shields fish quays, on the edge of Tynemouth.

Fitzpatricks, Front Street, is a handsome establishment. It is one of eight pubs in the small town. Has a changing selection of hand-pulled ales. Food served.

The Turks Head, Front St, otherwise known as the Stuffed Dog because of Willie the Scottish collie, whose 130 year old taxidermised remains sit in a glass box looking at the bar. Willie came down from the Scottish Borders with a herd of sheep and a shepherd, but somehow got separated from them and spent the rest of his life waiting and pining in Tynemouth for his lost master. A tale of epic proportions told in detail on a plaque. Good Courage Directors, regular guest ales. Food served all day.

Places of interest

Tourist Information Centre: TICNS@ northtyneside.gov.uk. 0191 200 5896 or 0191 200 8703

Sea Life Aquarium - more than 30 hi-tech displays provide encounters with dozens of sea creatures. Journey 'beneath' the North Sea and discover thousands of amazing sea creatures.

Black Middens - once notorious rocks near the Tyne entrance which in the 1860s claimed five ships in three days. Tynemouth Castle and Priory: dating from the 7th century, this was the burial place for the Kings of Northumbria but was later destroyed by the Danes. Later founded as a Benedictine Priory and later still fortified, but now a picturesque ruin.

Cycle shops

Whiptail Cycles
3, Livingston View,
Tynemouth, Tyne & Wear,
NE30 2PL
0191 257 2212

Dixons Cycles
184 Park View, Whitley
Bay, Tyne and Wear,
NE26 3QP.
info@dixons-cycles.co.uk
0191 253 2035

Accommodation

Marlborough Hotel, 20–21 East Parade, Promenade, Whitley Bay, NE26 1AP

Smart and comfortable sea front hotel in prime position in Whitley Bay with many of the rooms overlooking the sea. High standards of accommodation (the rooms were recently refurbished) and hospitality. Close to all transport links - secure bike parking plus drying facilities. There is now free WiFi throughout plus the use of a computer in the sitting room.
Rooms: 4S, 6D, 2T, 4F.
B&B: £25-£45 (negotiable for groups or longer stays).
Pk lunch: £5.
VisitBritain & AA 4 stars (guest accommodation).
0191 251 3628/F 0191 252 5033
www.marlborough-hotel.com/
reception@marlborough-hotel.com

Park Hotel, Grand Parade, Tynemouth, Tyne & Wear NE30 4JQ

Overlooking the Northumbrian coastline with fantastic views the Park is ideal for cyclists on any of the many routes that begins or ends around Tynemouth. There is a 200-space car park, ideal for leaving your car whilst off cycling. The restaurant has an extensive a la carte menu plus carvery and all food is freshly prepared on the premises. The 55 rooms, most of them with sea views, are all en-suite with tea and coffee facilities, satellite TV, direct dial telephone. There is an English breakfast eat-as-much as-you-like buffet.
Rooms: 46T/D, 4S, 5F, all but 5 of which have sea views.
B&B: from £37.50.
Evening meal: £5 carvery deal for cyclists. Sunday lunch or between 1700-1900.
Pk lunch: on request.
Secure indoor cycle storage. On route.
0191 257 1406
www.parkhoteltynemouth.co.uk
info@parkhoteltynemouth.co.uk

York House Hotel, 106–110 Park Avenue, Whitley Bay, NE26 1DN

Run by: Michael & Marissa Ruddy
Near start and end of C2C, Reivers and Coast & Castles. 100m to the nearest pub and 250m to the beach. Delightful family run hotel conveniently and yet quietly situated close to all amenities. All rooms are en-suite with fridges and microwaves. Secure indoor cycle storage.
Rooms: 2S, 5D, 3T, 3F.
B&B: £27.50-£32.50. Pl lunch: £5.95.
VisitBritain 4-star (guest accommodation)
0191 252 8313/F:0191 251 3953
www.yorkhousehotel.com
reservations@yorkhousehotel.com

Oaktree Lodge, 15 Esplanade, Whitley Bay, Tyne & Wear, NE26 2AH
Run by: Andrew Birds
Contemporary in design, yet still maintaining the unique
character of its victorian heritage. The 4 Star award winning
Oaktree Lodge is located in a quiet position central to Whitley
Bay and just 500 yds from Whitley Bay's beautiful beaches. Be
assured we provide the highest standards of quality, comfort and
service available in the Whitley Bay area.
Rooms: 4T, 1Tpl, 2D, 1 S.
B&B: £30.
Evening meal: £7.50.
Pk lunch: £5.
Secure bike storage. Free WiFi.
AA & Visit Britain 4 stars.
Licensed Bar. Modern coffee lounge
serving speciality coffees and teas.
0191 2528587
oaktreelodge@aol.com
www.oaktree-lodge.co.uk

The Northumbria, 51 – 52 Victoria Avenue, Whitley Bay, NE26 2BA
Run by: Christine Goodwin
Seafront position and splendid views. Friendly and welcoming,
Christine is a language teacher fluent in Spanish, French and
German. There's a secure lock-up and a laundry facility. The
Northumbria has eight cheaper hostel rooms plus six further
3-star bedrooms. Ideal for any of the routes coming into/leaving
the Whitley Bay-Tynemouth area.
8 hostel rms sleeping 2-4 in bunks; 2D, 2T, 2S
B&B: £15 for hostel;
£25-£35 (£35-£45 for single occ)
Evening meal: on request,
around £15 for 3-courses.
Pk lunch: on request.
Secure lock up Laundry
0191 252 5265
www.northumbria-hotel.co.uk
northumbriahotel@btconnect.com

Avalon Hotel, 26–28 South Parade, Whitley Bay, Tyne & Wear NE26 2RG
Run by: Michael Farwell
Ideal location: the Avalon is also a pub and is close to the start
of Reivers and Coast & Castles, and close to the end of the C2C.
Family run 3-star hotel with 14 en-suite rooms, secure bike
storage, fully licensed bar, plus washing and drying facilities.
Great breakfast and very cycle friendly.
Rooms: 3S, 6D, 6T, 3F.
B&B: from £30-£40.
Pk lunch: by arrangement.
0191 251 0080/F: 0191 251 0100
www.theavalon.co.uk
info@theavalon.co.uk

Directions

- Take good note: it is easy to get lost beyond North Shields. Start at the Spanish Battery Car Park by the cluster of arty waysigns below the Castle and Priory. Leaving Admiral Collingwood's fine statue on your right follow the cycle path to North Shields Fish Quays with its restaurants, fish and chip shops and old fashioned stores.
- There is a plethora of Route 72, Route 10 and C2C signs (you are also on the C2C). Union Quay becomes Bell St, Liddle St and Clive St. Follow the signs, which take you to Lowson St. At the end of Chirton Dene Way you need to skirt round to the right of Wet n'Wild indoor water park.
- Follow the path to the right, along the cycle path parallel with Coble Dene, opposite the shopping centre at Royal Quays, where the DFDS ferries come in. Turn left onto the cycle path following the busy A187. Take care when crossing it. A clearly delineated cycle path shortly takes you above the Tyne, past Segedunum Roman Baths & Museum, skirting Wallsend, Walker and Byker before you are reunited with the Tyne and the magnificent run into Newcastle.

Fish Quay is a vibrant little community of retailers who inhabit this scenic stretch. There are a couple of good pubs and plenty of places to eat, all commanding views of the Tyne. This is where Danish and Polish sailors used to come ashore to integrate vigorously with the local community at a den of iniquity known as the Infamous Jungle (this former brothel is now known as the Collingwood Buildings).

South Shields

Changing face of Tyneside

South Shields has six miles of coastline and three miles of river frontage, dominated by the massive piers at the mouth of the Tyne. One of the most striking features of South Shields (home of the romantic author Catherine Cookson) is its Town Hall of 1910, with its copper weather vane in the form of a galleon.

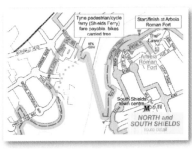

Airships raided the Tyne in World War I and the town's seafront amusement park was attacked in 1915. In World War II, it was much targeted by the Germans (156 people were killed in air raids). One direct hit on the market place killed more than 40 people who had taken shelter in tunnels below the square. South Shields also lost more seafarers than any other port in Britain during World War II.

The celebrated artist L S Lowry spent frequent periods at the Seaburn Hotel in Sunderland, and painted a number of works in South Shields. The town has also been home to a Yemeni community since the 1890s.

In 1977 it was visited by boxer Mohammed Ali, whose wedding was blessed in the local mosque at Laygate. Ali visited the town after receiving an invitation from a local boys' boxing club.

South Shields has undergone significant post-industrial economic change. The shipyards, mines, salt pans and glass making have been replaced by service industries, including tourism and retail.

Places of interest

Tourist Information Centre, Museum & Gallery, Ocean Rd, South Shields, NE33 2HZ. 0191 454 6612

Those interested in history will wish to have a good look at the supply base at **Arbeia Roman Fort & Museum**. Reconstructions, Life of a Roman Soldier exhibition and Death & Burial gallery are all part of this hands-on exhibition to show what it was like for the ordinary Roman soldier.

Open April 1 – Oct 31 1000-1700; Nov 1 – March 31 1000-1500 daily. Admission: FREE. 0191 456 1369.
www.Twmuseums.org.uk/arbeia.

Tyne Cycle Tunnel

The tunnel was opened in 1951 to service the shipyards and was once used by 20,000 people a day. The tunnel is 274 metres long and was the first purpose-built cycle tunnel. Tiled in elegant green and white, there is a red brick rotunda at each end and a distinct flavour of the recent industrial past. As it is a public highway, the tunnel is free and is open 24 hours a day. There is also a lift should the old escalator be out of service.

Bede's World Church Bank, Jarrow, Tyne & Wear, NE32 3DY

If you're taking your time (and we feel that you should), Bede's World (right) is well worth a visit. It is a lively celebration of the extraordinary life of the Venerable Bede (AD 673-735), who lived here 1300 years ago. The museum, next to the Tyne, has changing exhibitions. There's a good café in Jarrow Hall and a new museum building.
0191 489 2106
F: 0191 428 2361
info@bedesworld.co.uk
www.bedesworld.co.uk

Pubs

Alum Ale House, River Drive, NE33 1JR. Next to the ferry terminal. Claims to be the oldest pub in South Shields. But so does The Steamboat in Coronation St. 0191 427 7147.

The Maltings, Claypath Lane, NE33 4PG. One of the three pubs owned by Jarrow Brewery. Big and welcoming. 0191 427 7147.

Stag's Head, 45 Fowler St, NE33 1NS. Every Thursday there's a curry night. It costs £1. The pub has an award for its unchanged interior. It should get one for its prices. 0191 427 2911.

The Steamboat, Coronation St, Mill Dam, NE33 1EQ. Overlooks the Tyne (rather than the sea). Community pub. Claims to be the oldest in South Shields (see Alum above). 0191 454 0134.

St Mary's Lighthouse

Accommodation

Once upon a Tyne, 55 Beach Rd, South Shields NE33 2QU
Run by: Paul Taylor
Relaxed place close to the beating heart of South Shields. It's
a five minute walk to the beach and just a couple of minutes to
the fabled curry houses on Ocean Road. There are also some
fine old-fashioned pubs in the neighbourhood.
Rooms: 1Tpl, 1 quad, 2S, 2T.
B&B: £25.
Evening meal: dining room designed for mopping up takeaways.
There's a microwave and fridge.
No Packed lunch but a good sandwich shop nearby.
0191 454 3119
liveonce@once-tyne.co.uk
www.once-tyne.co.uk

Cycle shops

A-S Cycles 44 St Aidans Road, South Shields NE33 2HD
Tel: 0191 456 3133

Conway Cycle Centre 12 Salem Street, South Shields, Tyne and Wear,
NE33 1HH Tel: 0191 455 3579

Halfords Station Road, Millbank, South Shields, Tyne & Wear, NE33
1ED. Tel: 0191 4271600

South Shields – Newcastle

- If you opt for South Shields as opposed to Tynemouth the
  official start point is at Arbeia Roman Fort. However, many
  might wish to start at the mouth of the Tyne, just a mile or so
  east at Littlehaven Beach, where there are wonderful views of
  the harbour and Tynemouth Priory. The sandy beach is home to
  The Conversation Piece, a highly unusual work of art, next to the
  Littlehaven Hotel. Leaving the rotund sculptures behind, head up
  the gentle incline towards Arbeia, following the Tyne as it briefly
  courses southwards.
- If you wish to see the Arbeia replica fort you need to head
  up River Drive then left again and briefly into Mile End Road,
  turning sharp left into Green Place, then right into Baring St.
  Retrace your steps down to Wapping Street and head west along
  the Tyne, not forgetting to take in the wonderful views. You will
  pass the Spirit of the Tyne statue and the dry dock.
- Follow the signs and you will soon be at South Shields ferry
  crossing (£1.10 – bikes free for a seven minute crossing at 15
  and 45 minutes past the hour) should you wish to opt for the
  route along North Tyneside.

- Otherwise, simply carry on until Jarrow and cross at the Cycle Tunnel, next to Bede's World. This is a mostly urban section but with some good views across the Tyne before you reach the path next to the A194. You follow the main road for about a mile before taking a right turn just before Jarrow (clearly waysigned). You will be passing a ruined monastery of St Paul on the right before taking a left past Bede's World.
- This is where you should cross the Tyne, via the tunnel. There is a designated cycle tunnel running parallel with the pedestrian tunnel and the world's longest wooden escalator takes you down into the depths of the earth (60 metres). You link up with the route the other side, near Howdon Metro. The more people who use the tunnel, the more likely it is to stay open!
- You will now be linked up with the North Tyneside section of the route. For instructions (in the unlikely event you get lost), please see Tynemouth – Newcastle section.

Newcastle

Ancient 21st century Toon

Newcastle is far from new: its origins are Roman. It owes its name to the castle built in 1080 by Robert, eldest son of William the Conqueror. Wool was its business before coal took over. It became a port in the 16th century and soon shipyards lower down the river were established, later to become amongst the world's largest build

Newcastle/Gateshead attractions include: The Sage Gateshead, Baltic - Centre for Contemporary Art, Laing Art Gallery, Discovery Museum, Centre for Life and the Angel of the North.

and repair centres. In these post-industrial times the city is largely business and culture led, with a particular reputation for nightlife.

The medieval street layout still exists in large parts of the centre, with narrow alleys or 'chares', particularly around the riverside area. There are steps leading up from the Tyne to higher parts of the city and the Castle Keep, whose existence was first recorded in the 14th century. Close, Sandhill and Quayside boast some fine modern architecture alongside older buildings dating from 15th-18th centuries. These include Bessie Surtees House, the Cooperage and Lloyds Quayside Bars, Derwentwater House and the wonderful listed 16th century merchant's house at 28-30 Close.

Its late Georgian neoclassical centre, built in the early 19th century by John Dobson, was recently restored and vies with Bath for period splendour. Newcastle has been described as England's best-looking city and Grey Street, which curves down from Grey's Monument towards the valley of the Tyne, was voted England's finest street in a survey of Radio 4 listeners. Sadly a section of Grainger Town was bulldozed in the 1960s to make way for the atrocious shopping centre at Eldon Square.

Leazes Park, northwest of the centre, was built in 1873 as a "ready access to some open ground for the purpose of health and recreation" following a petition by 3,000 working men. Adjoining the park is St James's Park, home of Newcastle United, which dominates many views of the city.

Places of interest

Tourist Information Centre: Guildhall Visitor Information Centre, Quayside, NE1 3AF. 0191 277 8000, www.newcastle.gov.uk

8–9 Central Arcade, NE1 5BQ, 0191 277 8000

Segedunum Roman Fort, Baths & Museum
At Wallsend, just east of the city. This is a spectacular reconstruction of a fort which includes the bath house and a section of the wall, also offering a computer generated history tour and a 35 metre high viewing tower.
Open April 1 – Oct 31 1000-1700; Nov 1 – March 31 1000-1500 daily. Adults: £3.95, concessions £2.95. U-16s free.
0191 236 9347.www.Twmuseums.org.uk/segedunum.

Cycle shops

Cycle Centre 248 Shields Road Byker Newcastle upon Tyne Tyne & Wear, NE6 1DX.
0191 265 1472 sales@cyclecentreuk.co.uk, www.cyclecentre.co.uk

Cycle Logical
44 Forest Hall Road, Forest Hall. Newcastle upon Tyne - Tyne and Wear, NE12 9AL 0191 216 9222, www.cyclelogical-newcastle.com

Denton Cycles, 259 Scotswood Rd, NE4 7AW, Tel: 0191 272 338

Edinburgh Bicycle Cooperative, 5-7 Union Road, Byker, NE6 1EH
0191 265 8619, www.edinburgh-bicycle.co.uk (N.B. Formerly known as Hardisty's) 1 mile north of NCN 72 - via Byker Link and Shields Road

Recyke Y'Bike, Hannington Street, Byker, NE6 1JT
A community project that accepts donated bikes from members of the public and recycles them for use by priority groups of people, such as the long-term unemployed, those who have been homeless, and those with mental health problems.
Contact: Dorothy Craw.
07737 526020 F: 0191 292 9963,
www.recyke-y-bike.org

Accommodation

Full details in the C2C section of the guide: Pages 117-118

Clifton House Hotel, 46 Clifton Rd, Newcastle upon Tyne, NE4 6XH
0191 273 0407 / cliftonhousehotel@hotmail.com
www.cliftonhousehotel.com

**The Cumberland Arms, Ouseburn, Byker, Newcastle upon Tyne,
Tyne & Wear, NE6 1LD**
0191 265 6151 / info.cumberland@googlemail.com
www.thecumberlandarms.co.uk

Travel Lodge, 4 Forster St, Quayside 0191 261 5432

Newcastle – Wylam/Ovingham

- As you head out of the city with the urban sprawl of Elswick and Benwell on your right, gradually the countryside opens up. Watch out for fishermen blocking the path. At mile point 161 you will need to cross the busy Scotswood Road onto its north side, soon joining the rail path, only to cross back again two miles later, around the point where the C2C branches off for Rowlands Gill. Carry on towards Newburn, closely following the (well signposted) Tyne along a flat section.

- Soon you will be passing just south of Heddon on the Wall, a pleasant little village bang on Hadrian's Wall. This is worth a stop off as there is an excellent B&B and The Swan does a good and cheap carvery.

Eating

The Swan, Reliable and copious carvery. Other options in a neatly refurbished old pub.
01661 853161

Accommodation

Heddon Lodge, Heddon Banks, Heddon on the Wall, NE15 0BU.
Run by: Jacqueline Ryan. Heddon Lodge is in the heart of
beautiful Northumberland countryside and is a welcoming and
comfortable stop-off, ideal for exploring the surrounding areas
and for enjoying all the many attractions available. Very cycle
friendly.
Rooms: 3D
B&B: £37.50.
Evening meal: no – you go to the Swan.
Packed lunch: on request.
Secure lock-up, drying facilities. Geared up for the job.
01661 854042 or 07802 660485
info@heddonlodge.co.uk
www.heddonlodge.co.uk

Route

Just before Wylam you cross onto
the south side of the Tyne at Hagg
Bank until Ovingham, crossing bank
onto the north bank at Prudhoe
railway station. Please note that
there is no cycling on the footbridge
and be careful on the road bridge as
it's narrow and dangerous.

Take care on narrow bridge,
loop back under bridge to
join riverside path

Wylam

Steam makes way for pedal power

The loss of the Scotswood, Newburn and Wylam Railway was
the cyclist's gain: the HCW follow its course before taking
you through this picturesque Tyneside community, with its
own splendid little brewery. Wylam was the home of George
Stephenson, 'father of the railway', and his cottage is now
a bijou museum. The old line, needless to say, ran past its
doorway. On the opposite side of the river the Tyne Valley
Railway still operates between Newcastle and Carlisle.
Wylam has also been home to the novelists Margaret Drabble,
Lady Antonia (A.S.) Byatt, not to mention the former BBC boss
Greg Dyke. Charles Algernon Parsons, inventor of the steam
turbine, lived here, as did rail pioneers William Hedley and
Timothy Hackworth. It has benefited – as has the entire Tyne
Valley – from the recent prosperity of Newcastle.

Places of interest

Wylam Railway Museum, Falcon Centre, Falcon Tce, Wylam, NE41
8EE. Tues & Thurs 1400-1930; Sat 0900-1200. 01661 852174
George Stephenson's Birthplace, Wylam NE41 8BP.
19/3/09 – 1/11/09 1200-1700 Thurs, Fri, Sat & Sun plus Bank
Holiday Mondays. £2 adults £1 children. 01661 853457

Accommodation

Ovington House, Ovington, Prudhoe, NE42 6DH
Run by: Lynne Moffitt
Georgian house set in five acres of land with stunning views across the Tyne Valley. Built in the 1730s with original features, such as shutters and fireplaces, there is an orchard, courtyard and also a converted barn with open plan accommodation.
Rooms: 2T, 3D.
B&B: £35-£40.
Evening meal: restaurant near by
Pk lunch: please give notice.
Cycle friendly with secure lock-up
drying facilities
01661 832442
stay@ovingtonhouse.co.uk
www.ovingtonhouse.co.uk

Wormald House & local shop: 01661 852529
www.wormaldhouse.co.uk

Bistro–en–Glaze, restaurant with rooms: 01661 852185.

Ovingham – Corbridge

Never mind that Hadrian's Wall is a few miles to the north at this point. Roman troops would not have had anything like as good a view of the Tyne. Cross over Ovingham Bridge and hang a left into River View, going past the local school. You are now on the country lane that takes you north of Bywell, just past mile marker 148, going under the A68 near Riding Mill. There is a mile long climb here taking you from Styford Bridge past High Barns. The lane then takes you to a T-junction, where you head left and descend into Corbridge.

Tynemouth as seen from the Littlehaven start point.

Corbridge

Potted history

Corbridge is not just a pretty face, it is a real place. One of the most attractive towns in the north of England, it bustles with activity. Its name probably derives from the Roman 'coria', which means 'tribal centre'. Lying at the junction of Stanegate and Dere Street, it was a major Roman stronghold. The fort here was established

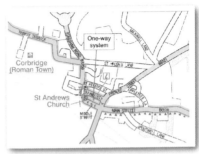

in AD 85 and by the middle of the 2nd century a town, with two walled military compounds, had grown around it. Some spectacular finds have been unearthed, including the Corbridge Lion and the Corbridge Hoard of Armour.

The parish church of St Andrew was consecrated in 676 and the first bridge across this broad and fast flowing stretch of the Tyne was built in the 13th century, though the current seven-arched structure dates from 1674. Corbridge, like many towns in the area, suffered during the border warfare in the area from the 14th century. Marauders, known as Reivers, behaved much like a completely unrestrained version of the Sicilian mafia (see Reivers section for gory details). Border warfare, at its height between 1300 and 1550, continued in one form or another for an unconscionable total of 400 years.

Having mentioned writers connected with Wylam I feel duty bound to do credit to Corbridge: the town boasts (in addition to South Shields) Catherine Cookson and Ruth Ainsworth, author of the Rufty Tufty Golliwog series.

Places of interest

For background: www.hadrians-wall.org. 01434 322002

Tourist Information Centre, Hill St (Easter until end of October). 01434 632815

Corbridge Roman Town (0.5 miles north west of Corbridge). Substantial remains. Granaries, a stone lion and the Stanegate Road. All comes to life with an audio tour. Open all year round. Admission: £4.50, concessions £3.60, children £2.10.
01434 632349
www.english-heritage.org.uk/corbridge

Cycle shops

Activcycles, 17 Watling St, Corbridge
info@activcycles.net
www.activcycles.net

Accommodation

The Golden Lion, Hill St, NE45 5AA.
Run by: Del & Linda Peel
Popular and well run town centre pub/hotel built from stones plundered from Hadrian's Wall. Grade II listed and former home of Lord Derwent-Wates, who was executed following the second Jacobite rebellion. Leaded windows, nice bathrooms, great charm. And to cap it all, a beer garden.
Rooms: 5D, 1T/Tpl
B&B: from £35-£50 (single occ)
Evening meal: £6.25-£9.95. Bar snacks and takeaway service.
Packed lunch: £5
Secure lock-up. Separate side entrance for residents

Fellcroft B&B, Station Rd, Corbridge, NE45 5AY.
Run by: Tove Brown
Well-appointed, stone-built Edwardian house. All rooms with private facilities and colour TVs. Quiet road in country setting. Excellent choice of eating places nearby. A large comfortable guest sitting room on the ground floor with tourist information, books, DVDs and a TV.
Norwegian, Swedish, Danish, French and a smattering of German spoken here. Also please note that we accept dogs on the premises.
Rooms: 1 T, 1D/F. B&B: £30-£35
Evening meal: no – plenty of restaurants in town.
Pk lunch: Yes.
Secure cycle lock-up. Drying facilities.
01434 632384
tove.brown@ukonline.co.uk
www.fellcroftbandb.com

Wheatsheaf Hotel: 01434 632020

Priorfield B&B, Hippingstones Lane, NE45 5JP: 01434 633179

The Hayes, Newcastle Rd, NE45 5LP. 01434 632010

Angel Inn, Main St, NE45 5LA. 01434 632119

Where to eat

The Corbridge Larder – Deli and coffee shop. Cavernous and copious. **01434 632948. www.corbridgelarder.co.uk**
Watling Coffee House, 11 Watling St, NE45 5AG. Smart but slightly offbeat hangout for those requiring anything from a coffee to a full meal. **01434 634820.**

Tea & Tipple, Market Place, NE45 5AW. Opposite the ancient church and popular with shoppers. **01434 632886.**

Corbridge – Hexham

Follow the one way system through Middle St and you will soon pass the Corbridge Roman site. It's only four miles to Hexham. Watch out for fast traffic joining and leaving the A69. Just beyond Anick the lane can get busy with commuter and industrial traffic. You should dismount to cross the busy road bridge into Hexham.

Hexham

Potted history

Hexham has just over 11,000 people and is one of the three major towns in Tynedale (along with Prudhoe and Haltwhistle). The town's beginnings lie in the establishment of a monastery by Saint Wilfrid in 674. The crypt of the original monastery survives, and incorporates many stones taken from nearby Roman ruins. Hexham Abbey dates mainly from the 11th century, but was significantly rebuilt in Victorian times. Other notable buildings in the town include the Moot Hall, the covered market, and the Old Gaol.

Like Corbridge and many other towns in the North of England, Hexham had its nose bloodied on many occasions during the border wars with the Scots. Amongst those to administer them was William Wallace, who burnt the town in 1297, though the abbey survived largely intact. Not to be outdone Robert the Bruce demanded (and got) a ransom of £2,000 some 15 years later, in 1312, in exchange for not burning it down.

During the Wars of the Roses Hexham was the scene of battle in 1464. The Duke of Somerset, who commanded the Lancastrians, was defeated and beheaded in the Market Place. Later the town played its part in the 1715 Jacobite uprising, when James Radclyffe, 3rd Earl of Derwentside, raised the standard on behalf of the Stuarts. For his pains he was beheaded after the battle of Preston.

Places of interest

Tourist Information Centre, Wentworth Car Park, Hexham NE46 1QE. 01434 652220. www.ukinformationcentre.com (then type in Hexham).

Further information: www.hadrians-wall.org. 01434 322002.

Hexham Abbey: the current Early English Gothic church largely dates from c.1170–1250. The choir, north and south transepts and the cloisters, where canons studied and meditated, date from this period. The east end was rebuilt in 1860.
The Abbey stands at the west end of the market place, which is home to the Shambles, a Grade II* covered market built in 1766 by Sir Walter Blackett.

Moot Hall: a 15th century building in the east of the market place, is Grade I listed but not open to the public as it is home of the museum department of Tynedale District Council!
Old Gaol: one of the first purpose built prisons in England, it was constructed in 1330 and is a Grade I listed Scheduled Monument. Commissioned by the Archbishop of York (clerics were also governors and warriors in these times). There is now a museum.

Old Gaol: one of the first purpose built prisons in England, it was constructed in 1330 and is a Grade I listed Scheduled Monument.

Places to eat

Saathi Indian Restaurant & Takeaway, 28 Priestpopple. With a growing reputation, much more restaurant than curry house. **01434 603509**

Thai Royal Orchid, 26 Priestpopple. Owners of the Royal Hotel are Thai and claim to serve the genuine article here. We have not inspected, but reports are positive.
01434 600585 , www.theroyalorchid.co.uk

Cycle shops

The Bike Shop
16-17, St. Marys Chare Hexham
Northumberland
01434 601032

Accommodation

Royal Hotel, 26 Priestpopple, NE46 1PQ.
www.royalhotelhexham.co.uk

Best Western Beaumont Hotel, Beaumont St, NE46 3LT.
www.bw-beaumonthotel.co.uk

Woodley Field, Allendale Rd, Hexham, NE46 2NB

Run by: Jean Charlton

Ideal for small groups, Woodley Field is an elegantly furnished ETB 4 Star rated B&B in the heart of Wall country. Built by an engineer who owned a local mine 110 years ago, Woodley Field's two large individually designed family rooms are decorated in keeping with the house, with magnificent views of gardens set back from the quiet lane to Hexham. White cotton bed linen, feather duvets and fluffy white towels are standard. Breakfasts are made from fresh local produce, and served in an oak panelled dining room with views of the gardens.

Rooms: 2F (1T, 1 sofa double, 2 further fold out beds. The other has 1D plus double sofa bed + 1 further fold out bed).

B&B: £40-£42.50 (no single occupancy).

Evening meal: 3 minute ride into Hexham

Pk lunch: on request.

Secure lock up. Drying facilities

01434 601600

woodleyfield@btinternet.com

www.woodleyfield.co.uk

Wall

Out of Hexham and a couple of miles up the A6079 road towards Chollerford, and the famous Chesters Bridge Abutment, is the Hadrian Hotel at Wall. This is a splendid pitstop, with excellent real ales and good cooking. You can link up with the route just beyond Chollerford and Walwick.

Accommodation

Hadrian Hotel, Wall, Hexham, NE46 4EE.

Run by: David Lindsay

Comfortable and cosy without being remotely stuffy. As a guest you can hunker down in front of the fire or go and have a beer in the lively public bar. The food is well executed and reasonably priced and the rooms are very comfortable without being expensive. A class operation at an affordable price.

Rooms: 2D, 4T.

B&B: £32.50-£36.

Evening meal: from £3.50 - £15.

Pk lunch: £5.50

Secure lock-up and drying facilities.

01454 681232

david.lindsay13@btinternet.com

www.hadrianhotel.co.uk

Hexham to Haltwhistle

(22Miles)

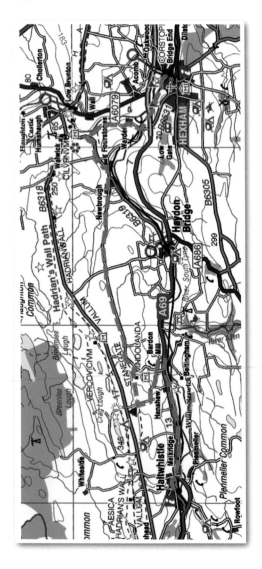

Directions

- There are two gated level crossings as you exit the town. Take care. You can also go directly to Fourstones but this is a narrow lane and therefore potentially hazardous as there are no verges. Instead, at mile marker 137, head up past Thistlerigg Farm. This takes you to Chesters Roman Fort, which is well worth a stop and is about one mile further than the left turn onto the B6319 which takes you down to Fourstones.

Accommodation

Mid-way between mile marker 130 and 129, at Grindon Hill where the Haydon Bridge lane connects with the Military Road, is a splendid and isolated stop-off:

The Old Repeater Station, Military Rd, Grindon, Northumberland
Run by: Les Gibson
Five rooms with a choice of bunk or en-suite twins. Charges are from £22.50 per person per night for a shared bunk bed room and from £30 per person per night for an en-suite room. This includes a continental style breakfast, or a full English cooked breakfast (supplement £3). Block bookings are also catered for (maximum 12 people). Ideal for exploring at leisure the treasures at Chesters, Housesteads and Vindolanda.
On-site parking. There is a guest sitting room with TV, Radio and DVD player, books, maps and guides, plus a garden with views over Sewingshield Crags.
Cycle storage
01434 688 668
les.gibson@tiscali.co.uk
www.hadrians–wall–bedandbreakfast.co.uk

Directions

- If not going to Chesters, turn left onto the B6319 and head down to Fourstones and be prepared: the steepest climbing is about to start along the Stanegate (old Roman road), once you get to Newbrough. There's a 200 metre ascent to the highest point on the route, Crindledykes (262 metres).

- A two mile diversion ahead takes you to Housesteads Roman Fort (Vercovicivm). For background: www.hadrians-wall.org. 01434 322002. A little further (steeply) down the route and then back up an equally steep section is is Vindolanda fort. Tea room and museum. Easier and quicker to access than Housesteads.
- You are in the heart of Roman Britain. You will also see signs for Route 68 at Smith's Shield. This where Pennine Cycleway and HCW conjoin. There is now a steep descent to Bardon Mill, where you go under the A69 before turning right.

Accommodation

Burnhead, Cawfields, Haltwhistle, NE49 9PJ

Run by: Dave & Christine Hunter
Bang on the Wall, Burnhead was built in 1830 from stones hewn by the Romans and was once the quarry manager's home. On one of the most stunning sections of the route, the quarry became defunct many years ago and the site has been beautifully restored showing a slice through the volcanic rock strata called the "Whin Sill" upon which much of the wall is built.
Rooms: 2T (en-suite).
Evening meal: quick walk up to the Milecastle Inn.
Pk lunch: £5.
Secure storage.
Hose down facilities and drying room.
4-star VisitBritain.
Cyclists Welcome scheme.
01434 320841
enquiries@burnheadbedandbreakfast.co.uk
www.burnheadbedandbreakfast.co.uk

Twice Brewed Inn, Military Rd, Bardon Mill, Hexham, NE47 7AN. . Three miles west of Haltwhistle. Accommodation and meals. 01434 344534

The Milecastle Inn is a wonderful pub on the corner of the Military Road and the lane leading down to Haltwhistle, so is a mile or so off the cycle route. But well worth a detour if you are staying nearby or planning to stop off for lunch, as the food is good, home cooked and reasonably priced. The owner, Kevin Hind, keeps a great pint of beer. There's a restaurant and a couple of old-fashioned bars and some great photographs and prints on the walls.
01434 321372

Haltwhistle

Potted history

Haltwhistle comes from Old English words Hal-twysel, meaning "a meeting of the streams by the hill". Twistle is a meeting of the waters and here the Haltwhistle Burn from the north meets the River South Tyne, thus making it a strategic

settlement for the Romans. The Wall is just over half a mile to the north, and much of the stone was quarried nearby.

On the Newcastle to Carlisle rail line, the town developed with the industrial revolution. In the 18th and 19th centuries coal mining was the main industry. Metal ores extracted from the mines on Alston Moor were also loaded here.

In 1836 workmen found a copper vessel containing 63 gold and copper coins with the minted heads of four Emperors: Claudius Caesar; Nero Claudius Drusus Germanicus; Nero and Vespasian. More recently, paint manufacture became a major commercial force in the town, but has now stopped major production. In the 21st century, the tourist industry dominates the economy, with Hadrian's Wall and walking and cycling counting among the principal interests of tourists.

Places of interest

Tourist Information Centre, Railway Station, Station Rd.
01434 322002

Church of the Holy Cross, below the Market Place with views over the river and the valley. 13th century and impressive for a modest town. Medieval graves.

Cycle shops

Edens Lawn Cycle Hire
By Pass Road,
Haltwhistle, NE49 0HH
tel: 01434 320443

Accommodation

Wydon Farm, Haltwhistle, Northumberland NE49 0LG

Run by: Linda Ogle
This is the only working National Trust farm in Northumberland which does accommodation. About a mile from Haltwhistle (there's a tunnel under the A69 to get to the farm), Linda will run you to the pub for an evening meal. You will sleep in smartly converted barns overlooking a courtyard.
Rooms: 2F (sleep up to 4), 1D (king size bed).
B&B: £32.50-£50.
Evening meal: Local pubs in Haltwhistle. Linda will provide transport.
Pk lunch: Yes.
Secure lock-up.
Washing and drying facilities
(Linda will happily wash your kit).
01434 321702 or 07808 208052
stay@wydon-haltwhistle.co.uk
www.wydon-haltwhistle.co.uk

Manor House Inn, Main St, Haltwhistle, NE49 0BS

Old coaching Inn (3 star rating) with good home cooked food, clean comfortable accommodation with lively public bar in the centre of Haltwhistle. Four en-suite bedrooms plus three more which share one bathroom, ideal for small parties. Food ranges from bar snacks to main meals served in the lounge area. Start your day with a full English breakfast, served in the restaurant. The bar has Sky TV, pool and games area.
Rooms: 6 rooms, all with tea/coffee making facilities, colour tv, hair dryer/ironing facilities upon request.
B&B: from £28-£39 per person. Discounts offered on minimum night stays and small party bookings.
Evening meal: £4.95 - £14.95 (Bar snacks - Main meals).
Pk lunch: £4-£6.
Secure storage and laundry facilities.
01434 322588
manorhouse@nicho73.orangehome.co.uk
www.themanorhousehaltwhistle.co.uk

Haltwhistle to Carlisle

(29 Miles)

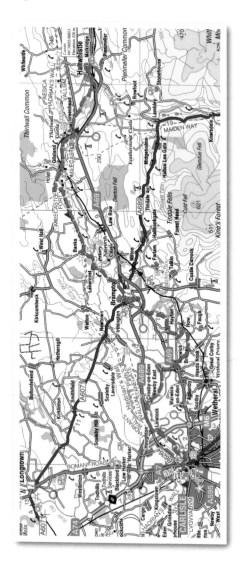

Haltwhistle to Gilsland (5 miles)

Gilsland

Potted history

Most of the 400 inhabitants live on the Northumberland side of the Poltross Burn and the River Irthing. Gilsland Spa has been a popular tourist attraction and there is a Spa Hotel, owned by the Cooperative Society. Sir Walter Scott visited in 1797 and later popularised it. After a whirlwind courtship with French émigré, Margaret Charlotte Charpentier, Scott is said to have proposed at the Popping stone. They married in December 1797.

Gilsland, originally an Iron Age settlement, has Milecastle 48 on its doorstep. Farming and mining were its staple businesses but now tourism (courtesy of the Wall) has taken over. Some 100 of the local inhabitants earn part or all their living from tourism and there are plenty of B&Bs.

Places of interest

Tourist Information Centre: 01697 747211

St Mary Magdalene's Church is set in beautiful rural surroundings. Early English Gothic style. Built and partially endowed by George Gill Mounsey who also erected what is now the Gilsland Spa Hotel.

Gilsland Spa, known in the past for its sulphurous spa waters, is close by.

Accommodation

Gilsland Spa Hotel, Gilsland, Brampton, CA8 7AR
Run by: Les Thompson
An historic tourist attraction (see history above). Extensive views over unspoilt countryside in all directions. Wander through the hotel grounds, which extend to 140 acres of peaceful park and woodland. Test the restorative properties of the Sulphur Well (if you dare). The Wall passes within a mile and a half of the hotel. Handy for the Vindolanda Museum and the Roman forts at Birdoswald and Housesteads.

Rooms: 4 F (sleep 3-5), 28D, 44T, 18S.
B&B: £42.50 (children under 10 1/2 price)
Evening meal: £8.50-£15.
Secure cycle storage. Drying facilities
016977 47203
reception@gilslandspahotel.fsnet.co.uk
www.gilslandspa.co.uk

Brookside Villa B&B, Gilsland, Cumbria CA8 7DA
Run by: Denise Collins
Licensed – serving good, locally brewed real ale or wine with your evening meal. Views are tremendous and the route passes the gate. The house is on the west side of Gilsland, sitting slap on the Cumbria-Northumberland border. Rooms have the facilities you would expect in a luxury hotel.

Rooms: 1F (sleeps 4), 1T/D. Beds zip and link so ideal for groups or couples
B&B: £30-£35.
Evening meal: £15 for 3 courses.
Packed lunch: £2.50-£5.50.
Licensed. Secure lock-up & drying facilities.
016977 47300
brooksidevilla@hotmail.co.uk
www.brooksidevilla.com

Walltown Lodge, Greenhead, Brampton, CA8 7JD
Run by: Diane Lowes
On both the Pennine Way and the Hadrian's Cycleway, Walltown boasts a brilliant location just off the B6318 the 'Military Road'. Warm Northumbrian hospitality in beautiful, cycle-friendly surroundings.

2D, 1T.
B&B: £30-£40.
Evening meal: from £15 (3-courses).
Pk lunch: from £5.
Secure lock-up. Drying facilities.
016977 47514
diane@walltownlodge.com
www.walltownlodge.com

Gilsland to Brampton (9 miles)

Route information

Follow the B6318 for just over a mile before turning left at Kiln Hill. This will take you past Birdoswald Fort. You will follow a three mile section of wall down to Banks Turret. There are great views to be had before heading down past Lanercost Priory (well worth a visit – there's a café and conveniences). Brampton is a further 3.5 miles.

Brampton

Potted History

One of the bigger conurbations, some 4,000 people live in this handsome sandstone enclave which nestles in a hollow gouged out during the ice age. There are several striking features to the town, among them St Martin's Church, famous as the only place of worship designed by the Pre-Raphaelite architect Philip Webb. St Martin's contains one of the most exquisite sets of stained glass windows designed by Sir Edward Burne-Jones, and executed in the William Morris studio.

On the outskirts of Brampton lies the Old Parish Church built, like so many edifices in the area, from Hadrian's Wall stone. In use until St Martin's was built in 1878, only the chancel now remains. Another fine feature is the octagonal Moot Hall, built in 1817. The Moot House has an external staircase to its upper entrance, pointed windows and a square turret. The building now houses the Tourist Information Centre. East of the town is an exceptionally large motte, about 135 feet high on top of which is a statue of the 7th Earl of Carlisle.

Places of interest

Tourist Information Centre, Moot House. 016977 3433.

Lanercost Priory is an absolute must, a romantic gem built in the reign of Henry II in around 1166. When completed in 1220, canons came from the priory in Norfolk. It was unceremoniously decommissioned by Henry VIII during the Dissolution of the Monasteries.

Cycle shops

Pedal Pushers
Lonnings End, Lonning, Capontree Road,
Brampton, Cumbria, CA8 1QL
016977 42387
pedalpushersbram@aol.com

Farlam Hall Hotel, Brampton, Cumbria CA8 2NG.

Farlam is 'the perfect place to escape from the real world and enjoy the elegance of a past era.' There are five family members working in the hotel supported by a team of 20. There are 12 luxurious en-suite bedrooms and a restaurant. Offers a style of hotel keeping that is becoming a rarity. Farlam is completely independent and is staunchly English, using fresh local produce and English products whenever possible.

Rooms: 6 D, 6T.

Dinner, Bed & Breakfast: £145-£170.

Evening meal: Award winning restaurant included in price.

Pk lunch: Yes.

Secure cycle storage. Drying facilities.

AA 3 Red Stars.

(Inspectors' Choice – Top 200 in UK).

2 Rosettes for restaurant.

Member Relais & Chateaux. Good Hotel Country House Hotel of the Year 2000-1.

01697 46234

farlam@farlamhall.co.uk

www.farlamhall.co.uk

Brampton to Carlisle (15 miles)

Route information

Pretty straightforward. You may wish to take the short cut to Warwick Bridge at Hayton. Otherwise follow the signs. HCW takes you through Newby East, Newby Grange and the attractive hamlet of Crosby-on-Eden, four miles east of Carlisle.

Accommodation

Crosby Lodge Country House Hotel & Restaurant, High Crosby, Crosby-in-Eden, Carlisle, CA6 4QZ.
Run by: Patricia and Philippa Sedgwick
Delightful, old fashioned and luxurious hotel tucked away from the path. Romantically castellated, this Georgian hotel stands above the village of Low Crosby, overlooking parkland and the river Eden. Built in 1805 as a family residence, which it still is today, Crosby Lodge is set in 4.5 acres of woodland and walled garden. Exciting menus, combining authentic continental cuisine with traditional British fare, acclaimed for desserts, home baking and preserves and a sensational wine list. Sunday lunch £28 per person Table d'hote four course dinner £39 per person. Light lunches from £6.75. Not for the budget traveler.
Rooms: 11.
B&B: £80. Secure cycle storage.
Drying facilities.
01228 573618
enquiries@crosbylodge.co.uk
www.crosbylodge.co.uk

Carlisle to Silloth

(35 Miles)

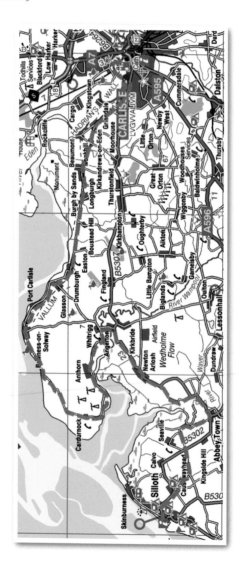

Carlisle

Potted history

These days Carlisle greets its guests with open arms, but not so long ago any visitor would have been treated with suspicion. It was the nerve-centre for bitter feuds and bloody battles created by the disputed Border. Early in its history it was a Roman headquarters for the Wall. In 1092 William the Conqueror's son William Rufus started to build the castle where later Mary Queen of Scots was incarcerated. During a period of Scots occupation its ruler was one Macbeth. Known as 'Carluel' it was, according to legend, the domain of King Arthur, and the Emperor Hadrian was perhaps the first to realize that whoever held Carlisle could influence the destinies of both England and Scotland.

You only have to look at the vast ramparts of the castle to realise the city's strategic importance. It is the home today of the King's Own Royal Border Regiment. If you get time, it is worth looking at its labyrinths to find the Licking Stones, so called because the water running down them was the only form of sustenance available to the Jacobite prisoners captured following Bonnie Prince Charlie's retreat in December 1745. The cathedral is also worth a visit. The city's long-running commercial success is celebrated in the Guildhall Museum, once a meeting place of the medieval trade guilds. Home of Carr's biscuits, its pubs were once nationalised to regulate drinking hours because of the massive (and dangerous) munitions industry which dominated the local economy.

Featherstone Castle near Haltwhistle

191

Places of interest

Tourist Information Centre, Old Town Hall, Green Market, Carlisle CA3 8JA. 01228 625600

If by chance you have cycled all the way from Wallsend and still need to know more about the Roman history of the Wall then before you leave Carlisle it is worth visiting Tullie House. This excellent museum will also give you a great deal of local information to help you on your way.

Cycle shops

Hollymill Cycles 140 Botchergate, Carlisle, CA1 1SH.
01228 513909

Palace Cycles 120 - 124 Botchergate, Carlisle, CA1 1SH
01228 523142

Rickerby's Currock Road, Carlisle, CA2 4BL
01228 27521

Scotby Cycles, 1 Church Street, Caldewgate, Carlisle, CA2 5TL
01228 546931

Whitehead Cycle Centre 128 - 130 Botchergate, Carlisle, CA1 1SH
01228 526890

Accommodation

Crown & Mitre Hotel, English Street, Carlisle, Cumbria CA3 8HZ
This splendid example of Edwardian architecture was built in 1905 on the site of the original Crown and Mitre Inn, and took three years to construct. Bang in the centre of Carlisle, amidst the historic sites such as Carlisle Cathedral, Carlisle Castle, the Old Town Hall, the Guildhall and Tullie House Museum. Refurbishments are now completed on over 50 of the guest rooms. The hotel welcomes cyclists and is a truly comfortable and stylish place to take a night off and rest your weary limbs.

Rooms: 16S, 78 D/T.
B&B: £35 (single supplement £20).
DB&B: weekend deal £45
(single supplement £20).
Secure cycle storage.
Excellent restaurant.
01228 525491
www.crownandmitre-hotel-carlisle.com
gm@crownandmitre-hotel-carlisle.com

Angus Hotel & Almonds Bistro, 14 Scotland Rd, Carlisle CA3 9DG
Run by: Martin & Rachel Perry
The foundations of the Angus are actually on Hadrian's Wall.
This is a small family run hotel offering personal hospitality, and
superb food in Almonds Restaurant. Licensed bar, secure cycle
store, drying facilities, packed lunches. Groups welcome.
Rooms: 2S, 5D, 4T, 3F.
B&B: £30-£52.
Pk lunch: £4.90.
Evening meals: £15 (3-courses).
On Reivers and Hadrians routes.
01228 523546. Fax 01228 531895
www.angus-hotel.co.uk
hotel@angus-hotel.co.uk

Langleigh Guest House, 6 Howard Place, Carlisle, CA1 1HR
Run by: Yvette Rogers
Highly recommended by many tourists organisations, private
road parking, five minutes from city centre, welcome trays,
spacious rooms. Ideal place to stop for a final night before
tackling the last stage.
Rooms: 1S, 3D, 3T, 1F.
B&B: £35.
Pk lunch: £5.
Evening meal £8-£25 (BYOB).
4 stars. Pub 5 minutes.
Lock-up/drying facilities
01228 530 440
www.langleighhouse.co.uk
langleighhouse@aol.com

Courtfield Guest House, 169 Warwick Road, Carlisle CA1 1LP
Run by: Marjorie Dawes
Comfortable, en-suite bedrooms, TV, tea/coffee facilities. Ten
minute walk to historic Carlisle city centre. Rightly famed for its
breakfast - a classy fry or fruit and yoghurt style options. Cycle
friendly and very well run.
Rooms: 1S, 3D, 2T, 2F.
B&B: £27.50-£30.
Pk lunch: £5.
VisitBritain 4 stars/Silver Award.
Pub 200m.
01228 522 767
mdawes@courtfieldhouse.fsnet.co.uk

Derwentlea, 14 Howard Place, CA1 1HR
Run by: Yvette Rogers

All rooms are en-suite and have tea and coffee making facilities and colour TVs. Warm Victorian house in a quiet conservation area with private car park and only five minutes walk from the city centre. Family rooms, cots, highchairs available; drying facilities; laundry service; secure lockable storage for bikes and equipment.

Rooms: 2S, 5T/D
B&B: £35
Eve meal: £8-£25 (BYOB)
Pk lunch: £5
Drying facilities/Safe storage.
01228 409706/07970 209760
www.derwentlea.co.uk
general@derwentlea.co.uk

Old Brewery Residences, Bridge Lane, Caldewgate, Carlisle CA2 5SR
Run by: Dee Carruthers

Accommodation in Youth Hostel rooms. All single rooms in self catering flats of 7 bedrooms. Total available: 56. All kitchens fully equipped, bathrooms have 2 wc/ bath and 2 showers. Bedrooms have bed, desk, wardrobe, wash hand basin. Bedding included. Towels to hire. Large lockable cycle store on site. Also excellent cycle shop 5 mins walk along road.

No meals available on site. But only 5 mins walk from town centre - with plenty of cafes/restaurants and supermarkets.

The Old Brewery is part of the Old Theakstons Brewery and sits beside the River Caldew, opposite Carlisle Castle, and is a student hall of residence for most of the year converting into a youth hostel during the summer months. A friendly team will welcome guests and issues keys and advice on where to eat etc. Once keys issued guests have 24 hour access.

Rooms: 7 - 56 beds.
Rates: £22 (£18 for u-18s).
01228 597 352
www.impacthousing.org.uk
deec@impacthousing.org.uk

Greysteads Private Hotel, 43 Norfolk Rd, Carlisle CA2 5PQ
Run by: Michael Potts

Elegant and old fashioned family run hotel in a quiet part of town yet within easy reach of the centre. Bedrooms all offer tea and coffee facilities plus TV and there's bags of parking space and a large secure lock-up area. Greysteads is on the way out of town heading south, towards the Dalston road and is right next to the route. Afternoon teas available.

Rooms: 2T, 2D, 1S.
B&B: from £30. Single occ. £40.
Pk lunch: from £4.
01228 522175
michael.potts@greysteads.co.uk

Aaron House, 135 Warwick Road, Carlisle, CA1 1LU.
Run by: Blanche Tiffin
Family run B&B, centrally heated,
en-suite facilities available, TV and
welcome tray in rooms, special diets
by prior arrangement.
Rooms: 1T, 2F.
B&B: £25-£30
Pk lunch: £4
Distance from Reivers: 0.5 miles.
01228 536 728

Hazeldean Guest House, Orton Grange, Wigton Road, Carlisle,
Cumbria CA5 6JB
Run by: Susan Harper
Friendly guest house with a unique attraction, 50m from Reivers
route: complimentary therapies available - massage, reflexology
and reiki. Spa suite, hot tub and sauna so ideal for an exhausted
cyclist. Large garden, secure parking for bikes.
Rooms: 1S, 2D, 1T.
B&B: £26-£28.
Pk lunch: from £3.50.
Evening meal: £7-£10.
On route
VisitBritain 3 stars /Pub nearby
01228 711 953
www.hazeldeantherapycentre.com
hazeldean1@btopenworld.com

Leaving Carlisle

Route information

The start of the next phase of your journey is along the close
planted borders of Castle Park. Enjoy these tree-lined avenues
because soon you will be out on the open marshes and
completely exposed to sun and wind for mile after mile. You
cross the River Caldew by a bridge built on the line of the Roman
Wall. Just around the bend of the river a new bridge over the
River Eden is planned, which will become the start of NCN Route
7 to Scotland.

Beyond the second
railway viaduct is
a steep flight of
steps which leads
you up to the area
known as Engine
Lonning, whose
ruinous ramblings
hide a fascinating
history. The wall
ran just a few
metres from the
top of the steps.

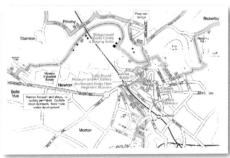

In 1823 the Castle Canal was opened from its basin here to Port Carlisle giving the merchants of the city a route to Liverpool. In 1853 the canal was drained and filled in by the Port Carlisle Railway Company. From here you have a virtually level journey for the next 87 miles all the way to Ravenglass.

The first part of the cycle route runs along the edge of the railway cutting, which is now even more filled in, but there are hopes to extend the route along the railway for another mile or so when the new Carlisle bypass is built. You join the road through Knockupworth and follow roads all the way to the Maryport Golf Club, 47 miles away.

©Countryside Agency- Photographer Simon Warner

Carlisle to Bowness-on-Solway

Accommodation

The Granary, The Old Mill, Thurstonfield, CA5 6HQ

Run by: Diane & Chris Veevers

Just over a mile south of Burgh by Sands.
Ideal base for exploring the Solway area, there is a minimum stay of three night at this one bedroom, 4 star, self-catering establishment. It sleeps two and has been lovingly and tastefully converted from the old granary loft adjoining the Old Mill. Built in 1774, the mill was a working water-powered corn mill until the early 1900s. There is an acre of lawn and woodland with a stream and a patio-barbecue area. In addition to the chickens there are lots of woodpeckers, sometimes common buzzards, swans and Solway geese.

Rooms: 1D.
Rates: minimum stay 3 nights £133-£210
Evening meal: self-catering + pub ¾ mile away.
01228 576205
diane@the-granary-thurstonfield.co.uk
www.the-granary-thurstonfield.co.uk

Burgh by Sands

Potted history

Burgh by Sands has numerous Roman remains. This was a vital strategic point, where troops were stationed to guard the two nearby Solway fords which were used by Scottish raiding parties. King Edward I (The Hammer of the Scots) died here on July 7th 1307, and his body was laid out in the village. The church is built on the site of the Roman Fort – Aballva. Out in the marshes you will find a sandstone monument erected in his honour, at the place he died whilst waiting to cross the river to subdue Robert the Bruce, King of Scotland. His long campaign resulted in considerable destruction and death in the Lake District and as a consequence local communities, determined to resist further massacre, built defensive structures known as Pele Towers. These included massive church towers here and at St Michaels at Bowness, which also doubled up as bell towers.

Accommodation

Hillside Farm, Boustead Hill, Burgh by Sands, Carlisle CA5 6AA

Run by: Sandra Rudd
Charming Georgian Grade II listed farmhouse with bunkhouse in a splendidly converted stable. Stunning views across the marshes and sands to Scotland. You can leave your car here and there's a secure lock-up.
Rooms: 1D/T, 1T
Bunkhouse: sleeps 12
£8 a night. Breakfast from £3; cooking facilities and pots/pans provided.
B&B: £28-£35
Drying facilities.
01228 576398
ruddshillside@btinternet.com

Route information

You continue along the line of the Roman Road to Drumburgh. The remains of the railway runs on your left and the wall, which was probably built of earth in this area, is over across the marshes on the right. When the new town of Silloth was created in 1854, with a deepwater dock into the Solway, the railway was again modified with a new line from Drumburgh through to Silloth. Then the construction of the Bowness-on-Solway Railway Viaduct so altered the deepwater channels that Port Carlisle silted up and was abandoned. The branch line though was maintained as a Victorian tourist route with horse drawn Dandy carriages from Drumburgh.

Accommodation

Hope & Anchor, Port Carlisle, Wigton, Cumbria CA7 5BU
Run by: Dougie & Liz Hill
Family owned country pub with home cooked food (Liz does the catering) and three real ales, mostly from a 20-mile radius. There's a secure lock-up and a boiler room for drying out kit. Part of the Cyclists Welcome scheme. Very obliging and right on the route.

Rooms: 1T, 1F (4 singles).
B&B: £25 (no single supplement).
Eve meal: £6.95-£7.95 mains
(about £12 for 3 courses).
Pk lunch: Yes. Flexible on this.
016973 51460
dougiehill@hotmail.com
www.hopeandanchorinn.com

Hesket House, Port Carlisle, Wigton, Cumbria CA7 5BU
Run by: Debs & David Hutton
'Nothing is too much trouble,' says Debs. This Grade II listed Georgian house was once the Steam Packet Inn when Port Carlisle was known as Fishers' Cross. Wonderful views in a wonderful part of the world. Woodrow Wilson, 28th President of the USA, once stayed at the Steam Packet.

Rooms: 1F, 2Tpl.
B&B: £28-£35.
Evening meal: the Hope & Anchor is only 100 metres away.
Packed lunch: £5
Secure lock up. Drying facilities.
016973 51876 or 07980 857086
stay@heskethouse.com
www.heskethouse.com

Bowness–on–Solway

Bowness-on-Solway was the end of the Wall and the most northern frontier of the Roman Empire after its withdrawal from the Antonine Wall between Edinburgh and Glasgow. The Bowness Roman fort of Maia was the second largest fort on Hadrian's Wall and the village is largely built upon its site. St Michael's Church is built over its granary. All the way along this coast there are sands and marshes and views across to Scotland well worth lingering over.

About half a mile on you pass the remains of the Solway viaduct, over a mile long, which crossed the river to Annan. The Solway Viaduct spanned 2544 yards and provided a direct route to Glasgow from the ore fields of West Cumbria and bypassed the congestion at Carlisle where seven railway companies, with seven engine sheds and depots, all jostled for space. The viaduct was repeatedly damaged by winter ice and was finally demolished in 1934. Local lore suggests that one reason for its closure was that the Scots, who at that time had no access to alcohol on Sundays, used to walk across to Bowness and occasionally fell off and drowned on their return trip.

Route information

Hadrian's Cycleway now follows the coast but you can take alternative short cut routes across to Whitrigg and Angerton. Newton Arlosh was created in the early 1300's to replace the village of Skinburness where the monks of Holme Cultrum

©Cycling for health day, photo by Rose Wolfe

Abbey panned for salt. This continued until the 1690's. If you visit the church of St John's note that the door is only 2 feet 7 inches high as it was built with defence in mind against the Border Reivers who were active at the time. It was said that at weddings the first of the bridal pair out of the church would be the boss.

Seaville was the home of the late John Naylor who constructed all the railway paths you will meet through Workington and Whitehaven. Whilst he was alive Sustrans had ambitions to construct a new route through the marshes to reach Skinburness and you might still like to take the main road through Calvo to pick up the Sea Dyke road to Skinburness for the full coastal experience. If you have time walk out to Grune

Point which is a noted spot for bird watching, particularly at high tides. If you are interested in war time defences, the Cumberland Machine Gun and Anti Tank Rifle Emplacement is a design of pill box unique to West Cumberland, whilst the Skinburness Mile fortlet formed part of the so called western sea defences, an extension of Hadrian's work which stretched from Bowness-on-Solway all the way down to Ravenglass.

Silloth to Workington

(23 Miles)

Silloth

Silloth was a planned town built in the 1850's around the new deepwater port. You will notice the wide tree-lined streets and the extensive sea front green, with magnificent promenade stretching back to Skinburness. Don't rush through Silloth. It has a memorable end of the road and edge of the land feel, and it's certainly not on the road to anywhere, so it might be a while before you come again. Its name derives from the "Lathes" or barns which were used to store grain and were located close to the sea, thus "sea lathes". The great English singer Kathleen Ferrier, for whom Benjamin Britten wrote several works, moved to Silloth back in 1936, when the town was booming.

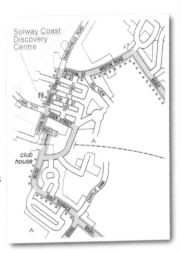

Places of interest

Tourist Information Centre, Solway Coast Discovery Centre (see below).

Solway Coast Discovery Centre, Liddell St, CA7 4DD (016973 31944). Film tour – shows coastal highlights. There are also frequent temporary exhibitions. 2006 marked the 40th anniversary of the Solway Coast being designated an AONB (Area of Outstanding Natural Beauty) and the Discovery Centre helps bring this to life with a fascinating montage of how the area developed from the Ice Age through to modern times. Lots of interesting facts about the Viking settlements here and the plethora of Viking place names.

For further information on the area, contact **The Solway Coast AONB Management**, Liddell St, Silloth, CA7 4DD.
016973 31944, www.solwaycoastaonb.org.uk

The Solway Coast AONB was designated in 1964 and covers 44 square miles (115 sq km) of the Cumbrian coastline between Rockcliffe and Maryport. It is one of 37 AONBs in England, which, like the National Parks, are protected as our finest landscapes.

Find out more about cycling in Cumbria:
www.cyclingcumbria.co.uk

Should you wish to spend more time exploring the **Solway coast**, take a look at the website www.hadrian–guide.co.uk for five wonderful cycle loops.

Places to eat

Cups & Saucers Farm Tea Shop, Seaville Farm, Silloth, CA7 4PT
Run by: Kathleen Hughes. Good spot to stop for a well-earned break. Open fire and even a hot tub. Mid-way between Abbey Town and Silloth.
01697 361256 www.croftlandscourt.co.uk.

Accommodation

West View Guest House, 9 Station Rd, Silloth CA7 4AE
Run by: Eileen & John Slack
Spacious en-suite rooms, cycle storage, free parking on road outside and bang on the route.
Rooms: 3T.
Rate: £22.50 bed only; £25 B&B.
£10 single occupancy supplement.
Evening meal: no – pubs and hotels nearby
Pk lunch: on request.
016973 31449
www.westviewguesthouse.co.uk

Route information
From now on the route diverts inland in order to avoid at least some of the rather fast coastal road, which we rejoin just north of Allonby. Intead of heading right onto the B5300 you carry straight on to the crossroads at Balladoyle, where you head right, passing The Gincase. If you do opt to take the B5300, take great care as it is a fast and narrow road with little or no verge. There are plans to have a cycle track and our website www.hadrian–route.co.uk will let you know when this project comes to fruition.

The Gincase, with its Farmhouse Tearoom, is an ideal stop-off, with a fine range of home baking and local produce. Serves morning coffee, lunch and afternoon tea which – weather permitting – you can enjoy in the orchard. There's a Craft Barn and a Gallery of local art, plus a farm park for the kids. The Gincase, Mawbray Hayrigg, Silloth, CA7 4LL. 016973 32020. www.gincase.co.uk.

Bank Mill Nurseries, Beckfoot, Silloth, CA7 4LF (01900 881340 www.bankmillnurseries.co.uk). It is on the B5300 just north of Mawbray and has a coffee shop, which does coffees, homemade soups, paninis and big breakfast baguettes, cakes and pastries, scones and sinful rum butter. There's also a fully licensed bistro open daily (except Mon & Tues) between 1800-2200 (last order 2100). There's a butterfly house and nature reserve.

Allonby

Allonby, among other things, boasts an exceptional ice cream shop. Once an important centre for herring fishing, in Victorian times Allonby became a coastal resort. Despite its modest size the village has several splendid buildings. Alfred Waterhouse, who also designed Manchester's Town Hall and the Natural History Museum in London, designed the Reading Room. Charles Dickens and Wilkie Collins are both reputed to have stayed at The Ship Inn whilst JMW Turner painted the sunsets from Silloth. In the 18th century this remote shoreline became a favourite place for landing contraband stored on the tax free haven of the Isle of Man. Near Allonby is Beckfoot (known as Bibra by the Romans). Coastal erosion here – hard by the B5300 – has exposed a Roman cemetery where urns and other artifacts are being rescued by English Heritage.

Accommodation

The Lowther Arms, Mawbray, Maryport, CA15 6QT

Run by: Dawn Lindsay

Perfect stop-off, just a few hundred metres from the beach and a couple of miles north of Allonby on the B5300. Offers B&B, camping, a static caravan and – from July 2009 – a holiday let. Varied menu offering home cooked lunch and supper made to order, using only the finest locally sourced and fresh produce. Real ales and a good selection of wines. Something for everyone and a real find in an area not over-endowed with accommodation.

Rooms: 1D, 1T. Also 6 berth caravan plus campsite with wetroom and electric hook-ups.

B&B: please call.

Eve meal: from £8.50

Lunches: everything from soup and sandwiches to full cooked meals.

Secure lock-up, drying facilities.

01900 881337

mail@lowther–arms.co.uk

www.lowther–arms.co.uk

Ship Inn, Main Rd. 01900 881017

Route information

Just before Bank End do stop off at the fortlet which has been excavated and gives you some idea of what this part of the Roman defence system looked like. It is also an excellent place to photograph the rest of your party cycling away down the coastal road.

At Bank End turn off the road through the golf club, who are very welcoming with refreshments, and join the promenade to Maryport. This point marks the start of long lengths of traffic free path. High on the hill above the promenade is Senhouse Roman Museum which can be reached by peeling off on one of the narrow tarmac paths leading to the Roman fort. Maryport was the command and supply base for the coastal defences of Hadrian's Wall and was occupied for nearly 300 years. The town was developed by Humphrey Senhouse in 1756, who called the town Maryport after his wife Mary. The Maryport and Carlisle railway opened in 1845 and the docks flourished, exporting rails and cast iron. They were the largest docks on the West Cumbrian coast until 1927, when Barrow was built.

Maryport

Maryport is a good place to stop, with an attractive centre, revived docks and new arts centre.

Places of Interest

Maryport Tourist Information Centre
Town Hall, Senhouse Street
01900 812101

The Wave, Irish Street , 01900 811450

The Wave is an imaginative and airy £3.3million Entertainment, Conferencing and Heritage Visitor Centre in the historic Georgian harbour of Maryport.

The complex features

Theatre, Concert Hall and Conference Centre

Interactive Heritage Visitor Centre

Bar and Café/Bistro

Gift Shop featuring 'Made In Cumbria' Arts and Crafts

Tourist Information Centre

Theatre & Cinema

The Main Theatre is a multi-functional space that will feature professional theatre and music performances, cinema, local community arts performances. There's seating for 234.

Heritage Visitor Centre

The Heritage Visitor Centre features interactive displays journeying through Maryport's past and promoting attractions in the town and areas of special interest. Learn about Ship Building in the town and Maryport's links with the Titanic. School Groups are also welcomed to the Heritage Centre, which offers an educational experience for all ages into the local industries of Maryport.

The Wave Café/Bistro

Offers light snacks, lunches, refreshments and a bistro menu in an agreeably light modern eating area. All food is fresh and homemade on the premises. There is a fully stocked licensed bar and a catering service for special events.

There's also a gift shop which stocks handcrafted gifts and artwork supplied by Made In Cumbria, as well as an extensive range of books.

Tourist Information Centre

The Centre also houses Maryport's Tourist Information Centre providing information on events, attractions and an on line accommodation booking system. So whatever it is you need to know – just ask.

www.thewavemaryport.co.uk

Lake District Coast Aquarium

The award winning Lake District Coast Aquarium, specialising in native British aquatic life, has some fantastic displays of our weird and wonderful fishy neighbours.

01900 817760 , www.lakedistrict–coastaquarium.co.uk

Maritime Museum

Shipping Brow

Tells the story of the docks, the town and Maryport's most famous inhabitants, such as Henry Ismay, founder of the White Star Line (of Titanic fame) and the family of Fletcher Christian, of the Mutiny on the Bounty.

01900 813738

Maryport Golf Club

Bank End, Maryport, Cumbria

Situated on the Solway Firth. Maryport golf club represents a unique golfing experience in Cumbria. You can enjoy a round of golf that is part traditional links and part parkland, whilst enjoying views of Criffel and South Scotland.

www.maryportgolfclub.co.uk

Senhouse Roman Museum

Housed in a Victorian Naval Reserve Battery this award winning museum houses the largest collection of Roman altars from a single site in Britain and lies adjacent to the clifftop fort of Alauna, part of the Hadrian's Wall World Heritage Site.

01900 816168 , www.senhousemuseum.co.uk

The Harbour Lights Project
Maryport Harbour
The Harbour lights project is a series of permanent
contemporary art installations set in and around the historic
harbour.
www.360spin.co.uk/artscouncil/maryport.htm

Where to eat

Captain Nelson, Irish Street, Maryport
open: Daily 11.30 am - 2pm including bank Holidays **01900 813109**
Cross Quays Fish 'N' Chips, 15 King Street, Maryport, **01900 815956**
Curzon Grill, Curzon Street, Maryport
open: Mon-Thurs 8.30am –9.30pm Fri & Sat 8.30am-10pm Sun 10am-9pm
Also Bank Holidays, **01900 819265**
Empire Coffee Shop & Sandwich Bar, Senhouse Street, Maryport
open: Mon-Sat 9am-5pm Wed 9am-4pm, **01900 817760**
Hong Kong (Chinese)
119 Crosby Street, Maryport
tel: **01900 812007**
McMenamins, Irish Street, Maryport
01900 819777, www.mcmenamins.co.uk
Pearl Garden Cantonese Cuisine, 44 Wood Street, Maryport **01900 818888**
Pedro's, 92 Senhouse Street, Maryport, **01900 816624**
Port of Call, Senhouse Street
open: Daily including Bank Holidays, **01900 810128**
The Lake District Coast Aquarium, South Quay, Maryport
open: Daily including Bank Holidays. Closed Christmas Day & Boxing Day
01900 817760, www.lakedistrict–coastaquarium.co.uk
The Lifeboat Inn & Harbour Restaurant
Shipping Brow, Senhouse Street, Maryport, Cumbria
open: Restaurant 7pm-9.30
0190010906, www.lifeboatinn–maryport.co.uk
The Wave, Irish Street, Maryport
open: Daily, **01900 811450**, www.thewavemaryport.co.uk
The Waverley Hotel and La Scalzi (Italian) Resturant
Curzon Street, Maryport
open: Mon – Sat 12pm –2pm 6.30pm- 9pm Sun 12pm – 2pm 7pm-9pm (La
Scalzi Closed Monday only), **01900 812115**

Accommodation

Waverley Hotel, 57 Curzon Street, Maryport, Cumbria, CA156LW
open: All year
5 double(s), 10 single(s), 3 twin, 2 family, 10 en-suite(s)
Family run hotel, close to pleasant harbour, town centre. Positive
reports of the food.
01900 812115

Route information and background

South of Maryport you will be following a purpose built cycle route nearly all the way to Seascale, south of Sellafield. This has been something of an heroic adventure occupying Sustrans, Groundwork and the Councils for the best part of the last 20 years. One recent addition is the new path south of the docks, past the reclaimed waste heaps to pass under the railway and on to Flimby. Ideas for a coastal route following the narrow strip of dunes between station and sea proved too difficult and you now follow an inland track to St Helens, and then a new roadside path past the Oldside and Siddick line of windmills on your right and the paperworks on your left, to join the start of a long series of railway paths.

The railway routes we follow are just some of the lines built in West Cumbria during a few frantic years in the mid 19th century. Coal was mined and exported by sea from 1650 onwards from Workington, Parton and Whitehaven, and early on horse drawn waggonways were made with at least eight lines in the Whitehaven area by 1820. We follow the one at Parton. The first railway here was the Maryport and Carlisle, built in 1845 by George Stephenson, and by 1850 the coastal line was open all the way to Furness. This all remains as the current mainline railway.

The route follows the lines built to serve the burgeoning steelworks. The Whitehaven, Clearwater and Egremont opened in 1866 and the diversionary line "Way of the Ironmasters", built to avoid the

punitive LNWR charges on the coastal route, opened from Siddick in 1879. But by 1880 the industry was already on the wane, the fabulous haematite mines worked out and the Ironmasters were importing Spanish ores. Gradually the mines closed – the last was an ore mine at Beckermet in 1982, and the last coal mine, Haig Pit at Whitehaven, in 1986. By then most of the inland railways were closed. This decline was the cyclist's good fortune and some 30 miles are incorporated into Sustrans C2C Routes, which themselves then became a catalyst for the whole National Cycle Network. As you cycle along these green and tranquil paths it is difficult to imagine the industry of every description which worked here scarcely 100 years ago, and all the more incongruous because of the area's association with the Lake District.

Workington

Starting at Siddick on the "Way of the Ironmasters", the land was all reclaimed from the sea. The lake on your left was original sea marsh. Beyond the lake above the sea cliff runs the railway path to Seaton and Cockermouth, part of the C2C route, covering the site of the Burgh Walls coastal fort now buried by the railway embankment. In the early stages of planning this cycle route Sustrans proposed the construction of a replica catapult to fire Hillman Imps over the lake to crash in a heap of ruined cars on the lower railway! The hills on the right, the seaward side, are in fact slag heaps and if you come across Jem Southam's recent photographic exhibition you will see how extraordinary this artificial coastline is. Just south of the junction between the two railway paths the route curls backward and forwards in a landscape sculpture designed by Mark Merror to create a point of interest in this derelict cutting. As you cross the River Derwent you will see a branch running along the river. This was opened to Cockermouth (1847), and if you follow this you will come to the lighthouse which forms the start of this branch of the C2C, with its panoramic view of the Lakes.

A potted history

Once the centre of the steelmaking industry, Henry Bessemer developed his revolutionary blast furnace here in 1857; at one stage its rolling mills produced rails for railways in almost every country in the world. By 1909 all the local works – Maryport, Oldside, Derwent, Moss Bay and Harrington – had merged into the Workington Iron and Steel Co. and after a final hectic period through the Great War the industry was worked out. From 1930 a single integrated "Combine" survived at Workington, but the last Bessemer "blow" was in 1975, the blast furnace shut down in 1982, and the rolling mills in 2007, when the work was transferred to Scunthorpe.

If you have time to wander down to the coast you will walk below a wholly man-made cliffscape, where the sea beats against slag and the detritus from making rails sent all over the world from Bolivia to India, and from Scotland to Capetown. Echoes from the steel heart of Britain's industrial zenith.

Accommodation

Route information

- In Workington itself the route runs through a car park on the old station site, which makes a convenient stopping point for shopping, before continuing to Distington. Here the once tranquil railway path has been blighted by the new A595 trunk road and the route that you follow is the result of long and not wholly satisfactory battles with the Highways Agency.

- You pass briefly through Lowca where coal was mined for centuries, locomotives were manufactured and a chemical works set up to develop coal by-products in 1911. This was famous for being shelled by German submarines in 1915. You rejoin the coast at Parton, below yet another Roman fortlet. It is worth stopping here to reflect that this minute cluster of buildings started life as an anchorage used by the Romans. By Elizabethan times small merchant vessels were trading from here carrying Moresby's coal to Chester. A cluster of industries developed in this little valley including saltpans, glassworks, the Lowca Engineering Company, which made the first locomotive for the Maryport and Carlisle Railway, which had to be shipped north by barge. There was also a large tannery squeezed in, but soon the whole area was taken over by a colliery which mined through the Parton Drift Tunnel, carrying the coal away by horse drawn waggonway to Whitehaven Port.

- We follow this tramway for a quite magnificent section of the ride with views north on a clear day to the Galloway Coast, above the mainline railway cut into the cliff below, right above the sea.

Workington to Ravenglass

(23 Miles)

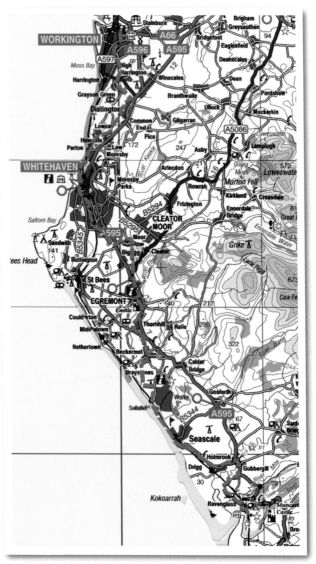

Whitehaven

Whitehaven is a highlight and is discussed elsewhere as the start of the C2C. Don't rush through, but enjoy the Georgian planned town, with its redeveloped harbour, the Beacon Visitor Centre, and the Haig Colliery Mining Museum high on the cliffs above the town.

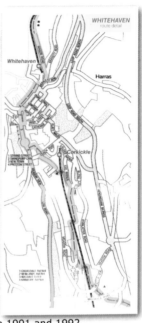

From Whitehaven to Moor Row Hadrian's Cycleway follows the line of the original C2C route opened in 1994. Notice the two seats constructed from bridge beams. The first of these is positioned exactly on the line of the railway with the beams 4 foot 8 and a half inches apart where they hit the ground to reflect the original gauge of the railways. The path diverts around the seats with the result that you get a wonderful view looking up the railway.

To mark each mile large rocks were brought in at the time of construction and positioned to reflect local history or interest. This route was built by Sustrans and Groundwork in 1991 and 1992 and considerable effort was placed on drawing in the local communities along the route by means of public art and other items of interest.

You will pass a number of steel way markers, all created by local schools under the guidance of Richard Farrington. At Moor Row the signpost consists simply of a whole school classes names, but all to the same purpose of giving character to the route and ownership to locals to win their support and care for it. Just before passing under the main road bridge you can divert away onto the minor road to St Bees (for accommodation in St Bees (see below) which is the start of Wainwright's Walk and would have also been a start of the C2C route had it been possible to construct a new path parallel to avoid the railway on this hilly road.

Just beyond Moor Row the route splits in all directions. Go to the left and you soon come to the Lady Victoria Mine which reputedly took coal, iron and limestone from the same shaft and now is surmounted by the Rock Crusher sculpture. Go straight on and you are on the way to Consett and Sunderland. Continue right along our route on the line of the Whitehaven,

213

Cleator and Egremont Railway, and you pass a number of interesting bridges.

First under the path runs a pedestrian tunnel where you walk on steel plates under which the Beck runs – a double deck bridge! You then cross over an old footbridge relocated from Egremont station and then under an elegant elliptical arch before rejoining the road. On the way you cross Wainwright's Coast to Coast Walk from St Bees to Robin Hoods Bay. Stop here at the junction to Cleator Village to take in the vista of the Lakeland hills and Dent Fell laid out before you.

Accommodation

Places to stay (For full details see page 18-20)

The Mansion, Old Woodhouse, Whitehaven, Cumbria CA28 9LN
01946 61860/01946 691270, comnenus4@aol.com
www.themansion–whitehaven.co.uk

Glenfield Guest House, Whitehaven, Cumbria, CA28 7TS
01946 691911, www.glenfield–whitehaven.co.uk
glenfieldGH@aol.com

Chestnuts, Low Moresby, Whitehaven, Cumbria, CA28 6RX
01946 61612, owlmagic@tesco.net
www.chestnuts–whitehaven.com

Glenard Guest House, Inkerman Terr, Whitehaven, CA28 7TY
01946 692249, info@glenard.co.uk
www.glenard.co.uk

Tarn Flatt Barn, Tarn Flatt Hall, Sandwith, Whitehaven CA28 9UX
01946 692162, stay@tarnflattfarm.co.uk
www.tarnflattfarm.co.uk

Chase Hotel, Inkerman Terrace, Whitehaven CA28 8AA
01946 693656 / 01946 590807, www.chasewhitehaven.co.uk
chase1@tms–connect.co.uk

Read Guest House, 5 Cross St, Whitehaven, CA28 7BX
01946 61515 or 07771 553819
ukbsolutions@msn.com

Waverley Hotel, Tangier St, CA28 7UX
01946 694337, www.thewaverleyhotel.co.uk
thewaverleyhotel@hotmail.com

Egremont (& St Bees)

The route in and out of Egremont has been a bit of a saga. First the Wood End link involved four separate land agreements, and a new bridge over the main road, and still the final link into town has to be pushed through unsupportive developers.

EGREMONT
route detail

Egremont itself is an interesting market town. The Vikings built a fort here and its Norman name it thought to derive from their town of Aigremont. Robert the Bruce sacked Egremont in 1322, resulting in a huge death toll. Lowes Court Gallery, on the main street, is the Tourist Information Centre and has a constantly changing exhibition programme. Stock up here on food and supplies for the last swing down to Ravenglass.

Places of interest

Lifted above the town 'like the Ark in the wilderness' the Norman Castle has fine herringbone stonework and views across the town, to Dent Fell and across to Florence Mine, which was the last deep iron ore mine in Europe.

Clintz Quarry Nature Reserve has such a remarkable and unusual diversity of habitats, ranging from bare rock to limestone woodland, that it became a Site of Special Scientific Interest 40 years ago. This status was awarded because of its plant life although the geology at the quarry would almost certainly qualify in its own right.

Stone House Farm, Main St, St Bees, CA27 0DE
Run by: Carole Smith

Secure bike storage On route for C2C and Hadrian's Cycleway Friendly family run bed and breakfast in a large modernised Georgian farmhouse in the centre of the village, near the railway station and local shops, restaurants and hotels. Only three minutes' ride from the start of the C2C (not to mention Wainwright's coast to coast walk). Full English breakfast and free parking. There is, however, a charge for long stay car parking of £2.50 per night.

Rooms: 1S, 2T, 1F 2D, 1Tpl.

B&B: £30-£35.

Evening meal: local pubs and hotels.

Pk lunch: £5.

01946 822224

www.stonehousefarm.net

csmith.stonehouse@btopenworld.com

Horse & Groom, Market Place, Court, Egremont CA22 2AE
Run by: Rob Merrett

Right in the town centre, in the centre of the Western Lakes, the Horse & Groom offers budget en-suite accommodation for families, walkers and cyclists. It is self-catering and there are plenty of shops, pubs and restaurants nearby. There is a secure lock-up for bikes and cleaning facilities.

Rooms: 1 six bed dorm, 1Q, 3T.

All en-suite wet rooms: £8.

Self-catering or surrounding pubs and restaurants.

Sleeping bags for hire £2

01946 758198

www.horseandgroomcourt.co.uk

info@horseandgroomcourt.co.uk

Albert Hotel, 1 Finkle St, St Bees, Cumbria, CA27 0BN
Run by: Carole

Clean and well run hotel at the bottom of Main St. A popular pub as well, with a pleasant beer garden. Carole obviously loves her job and the atmosphere is as warm as a steak pie. Secure storage and whopping breakfasts. Astonishing value and very tidy rooms, all with Georgian sash windows.

Rooms: 2D, 3T, 2S.

B&B: £25 (there is no extra charge for single occupancy).

Evening meals: yes for groups or those coinciding with groups. Around £4.50

Packed lunch £3

01946 822345

Platform 9 Restaurant & B&B, The Old Station House, Main St, St Bees, Cumbria CA27 0DG

Charming location at the start of the route with a good restaurant and a beer garden. There are three rooms and lots of restaurant choice, from bar snacks to a la carte. Chef Martin Allison had two AA rosettes. Secure storage for bikes. Great place to start from.
Rooms: 2D, 1T.
B&B: £32.50-£45.
DB&B: £75 (for two, weekend only).
Evening meal: £7.95-£19.95.
Pk lunch: £4.75.
01946 822600
stuart@platform9.co.uk
www.platform9.co.uk

Queens Hotel, Main St, St Bees, Cumbria, CA27 0DE

Run by: Mark Smedley

17th century hotel with a cosy country pub atmosphere: oak beams and log fires in the winter. There are two real ale bars and a decent wine list. The restaurant has been comfortably and tastefully refurbished and all meals are cooked on the premises using locally sourced ingredients where possible. Large conservatory and terraced garden. Secure cycle storage.
Rooms: 7 rooms currently available. A further 7 being refurbished.
B&B: £26-£38.
Evening meal: from £6.95.
Pk lunch: from £5.95
01946 822287
www.queenshotelstbees.co.uk
enquiries@queenshotelstbees.co.uk

Fairladies Barn Guest House, Main St, St Bees, Cumbria CA27 0AD

Run by: Will & Nicola Corrie

Beautiful 17th century sandstone barn that looks as if it has been transported from one of those picture postcard villages in the Dordogne. Luxury accommodation at affordable prices.
Rooms: 4D, 3T, 2F (1D & 1T with shared bathroom).
B&B: £30-£40.
Evening meal: lots of nearby pubs.
Pk lunch: £5.50.
01946 822718
www.fairladiesbarn.co.uk
info@fairladiesbarn.co.uk

Route information

Now on to Thornhill, beside the trunk road, for a short section of railway path which slots through a gap in the houses and beside a garage yard, for minor roads to Beckermet – at the meeting of Black Beck and Kirk Beck.

Seascale

Go straight if you want to get some idea of the size of the Sellafield operation. Sadly they have closed their visitor centre. Or go right to pick up the final section along the diversionary railway and the coast again at Sellafield marshalling yards and pick up the path through the dunes to Seascale.

This last traffic free section is particularly magnificent, confined as it is between the railway and the sea. Here Sustrans have introduced a variety of techniques to produce a narrow path which gives a memorable ride through the shifting sands.

Seascale is another coastal resort which flourished as a result of the Victorian Furness Railway (1850). The beach is magnificent and empty, and at some states of the tide is firm enough to cycle on if you are so inclined.

Accommodation

Calder House Hotel, The Banks, Seascale, CA20 1QP.

Run by: Andy Gainford & Steve Ainley

An imposing Victorian former girls' boarding school, perched above the sands seven miles from Ravenglass. Calder House is now a charming, old-fashioned, well-run seaside hotel with good beers, well priced and well chosen wines, and a competitive and inviting menu. Great value and a real throw back to the Edwardian era.

Rooms: 4T, 12D.

B&B: £30-£40.

Secure lock up.

Tel: 01946 28538

info@calderhouse.co.uk

www.calderhouse.co.uk

Sella Park House Hotel, Calder Bridge, Seascale, Cumbria CA18 1DW
16th century manor house hard by Calder Abbey with 11 rather
tastefully refurbished (and modernised) bedrooms. Six acres
of grounds, bar, snug room and home baked cakes and scones.
Good and local real ales, fine seasonal cooking using local
produce many of which are from Muncaster Castle's kitchen
gardens.
Rooms: Mostly twin and/or double
Rates: Rates: from £30-£60 per person. Ask about offers.
Evening meal: bar meals and restaurant where main courses
average £14.
Secure cycle storage.
01946 841601 or 0845 450 6445
info@penningtonhotels.com
www.penningtonhotels.com

Gosforth

One of these days the long awaited cyclepath from Seascale to
Gosforth will be completed, linking the vibrant and scenic village
to Hadrian's Cycleway. It is just over two miles along the B5344
to get to Gosforth, but the road is far from ideal, so be warned.
Gosforth has much needed accommodation and a couple of excellent places to eat, so provides an ideal alternative to Ravenglass for a last or first night stopover.
     On the edge of the Western Lakes, set within the Cum-
brian National Park and close to the Wasdale and Eskdale valleys
(not to mention the beautiful coastline). The village is a popular
destination for those wishing to explore this quiet corner of the
lakes.

Where to eat

Gosforth Hall Inn (see accommodation). **019467 25322.** Home cooking,
quality at reasonable prices.
Lakeland Habit, Main St, Gosforth. **019467 25232**. Excellent daily specials
(£5.95) in a comfortable 1st floor restaurant/tearoom. Run by Jonathan
Stanley and David Ancell, also good baking. **info@thelakelandhabit.co.uk.**
Westlakes Hotel & Restaurant.
019467 25221, www.westlakes.com
Gosforth Bakery Ltd, Meadow View, Gosforth. **019467 25525.** Gill
Unsworth has built a splendid business out of the small bakery. Great pies,
ideal lunch snacks.

Gosforth Hall Inn, Gosforth, Cumbria CA20 1AZ.

Run by: Rod & Barbara Davies

17th century hall of unspoilt charm, this is a gem of a place. The rooms are comfortable and log fires lend to the ambience. Runner-up in the Camra pub of the year 2008, the homemade pies are an increasingly popular feature. A great deal of effort from Rod and Barbara over the last eight years has gone into making this wonderful old building a comfortable and successful old-fashioned country inn.

Rooms: 9 D/T.

B&B: from £40.

Evening meal: from £9.95

Pk lunch: yes.

Secure lock-up.

019467 25322

info@gosforthhallinn.co.uk

www.gosforthhallinn.co.uk

Drigg

Drigg is the site of the UK 's Low Level Radioactive Waste Depository, situated about half a mile from the shoreline. As this is eroding at the rate of one metre a year it would seem to have a limited life. This whole area suffered greatly in the depression of the 1920's and 30's. So much so that Government industrial grants were given to bring in manufacturing, including the vast munitions works at Sellafield, which then became the Windscale and Calder Hall Atomic Power Station – Britain's first. Holmrook Hall nearby was requisitioned during the war, christened HMS Volcano and used as a secret training school to teach munitions and explosive demolition techniques for the Royal Navy, all under the disguise of a recuperative hospital for those suffering from shipwrecks.

If the weather is fine, turn off at Drigg to follow the as yet unreconstructed bridle path across the fields for the ancient packhorse bridge over the Irt.

Refreshments: Kathleen Egglestone, Spindle Craft, Drigg Station, Holmrook, CA19 1XQ. Coffee and cake just before you get to Ravenglass. Charming gift shop.

Accommodation

Victoria Hotel, Station Rd, Drigg, CA19 1XQ

Run by: Sandra & Peter Smith

Log fires, home-cooked food, real ale. You can leave your car. Warm atmosphere and secure lock-up. All rooms have en-suite shower and toilet and are supplied with hair-dryer, tea and coffee making facilities and colour television. The Hotel is located in the village of Drigg on the Cumbrian Coast and was originally built to service the railway that runs along the coast from Barrow-in-Furness to Carlisle

Rooms: 6D, 1F.
B&B: £40 per room.
Evening meal: around
£13 for 3 courses.
Pk lunch: yes
019467 24231
pjsmith2003@aol.com
www.victoriahoteldrigg.com

Ravenglass

This avoids the main road and brings you through to Saltcoats and a tidal path to the Mite Bridge attached to the railway structure. Hopefully here you will have time to look at the remains of the Roman bath house, once part of the base for the Roman Wall Fleet. Even better continue along the edge of the Esk Estuary and cross the river at low tide on the line of the Roman Ford, where the railway viaduct now stands. (If you are starting here then travel to Bootle Station and from there cycle north past the gunnery ranges for the whole military experience). Try to leave time for the Ravenglass and Eskdale Railway, which despite running on a 15in gauge, carries bicycles and leads you to the 8.5 mile Eskdale Trail waymarked route back from Dalegarth Visitor Centre to Ravenglass.

You can end on a suitably Roman note by visiting Muncaster Castle. This spectacular edifice has been in the Pennington family since 1208 and was built on Roman foundations. Ravenglass is the National Park's only coastal settlement and you may find that walking along the beach is a welcome break after 174 miles in the saddle. Stick around and enjoy!

Accommodation

Ravenglass Camping and Caravanning Club, Ravenglass, CA18 1SR
Member of the Camping & Caravanning Club. £8.17pp for campervans; £7.49 pp for tents.
Full facilities plus a shop.
01229 717 250

The Bay Horse, Main Street, Ravenglass, Cumbria, CA18 1SD
Run by: Elaine Gissing
Attractively and authentically restored 1764 house which Elaine and Mike spent 18 months working on before opening in May 2008. Old beams and wooden lintels now in evidence, along with warm hospitality and a generous Cumbrian breakfast. The stables have now been converted into living accommodation but part of it is now the Games Room, containing a half sized snooker table, darts board and board games.

Rooms: 2D. 1S
B&B: £27.50-£35
Evening meal: pubs up the road.
Pk lunch: £5.
secure storage.
01229 717015
mike.elaine@bayhorseravenglass.co.uk
www.bayhorseravenglass.co.uk

Pennington Hotel, Main St, Ravenglass, Cumbria CA18 1SD

Highly contemporary feel to this stylish old establishment next to the sea. Tastefully refurbished, the emphasis is upon unfussy comfort and good food (AA rosette). There's a bar serving bar food and a courtyard with an ice-cream parlour. Worth enquiring about offers.
Rooms: 2F, 16 D/T, 3D.
Rates: from £30-£60 per person. Ask about offers.
Evening meal: bar meals and restaurant where main courses average £14.
Secure cycle storage.
01229 717222 or 0845 450 6445
info@penningtonhotels.com
www.penningtonhotels.com

See also **Pennington Lodgings**, three Georgian houses in Ravenglass, plus The **Coachman's B&B** at nearby Muncaster Castle, which sleeps 29.
0845 450 6445.
info@penningtonhotels.com;
www.penningtonhotels.com.

Places to eat

Pennington Hotel
01229 717222. Upmarket and smartly refurbished.
Ratty Arms, Ravenglass, Cumbria CA18 1SN Tel: **01229 717676.** Busy and reasonably priced pub in the former Victorian railway station.

Beautiful Muncaster Castle

Morven House Hotel
Siddick Road
Workington
Cumbria
CA14 1LE
Tel/Fax 01900 602118

Relaxed and informal atmosphere for guests. En-suite rooms. Good food. Ideal stopover for C2C, Hadrian's or Reivers trail participants. Start your tour in a comfortable, detached house with car park and secure bicycle storage You may leave your car until you return, if you wish.

CYCLING HOLIDAYS ON THE C2C, REIVERS AND HADRIAN CYCLE ROUTES

Do you need help with transport, baggage transfers or accommodation?

Accommodation to suit your needs, preferences and budget. Any duration (usually 3-7 days). All year round holidays or as an individual back-up service to your own arrangements

Phone or fax 0191 284 7534
Ted Gillman at TYNE VALLEY HOLIDAYS